Self-Conf

Unleash Your Hidden Potential and Breakthrough Your Limitations of Confidence

Copyright 2017 by Bill Andrews - All rights reserved.

This document is geared towards providing exact and reliable information in regards to the topic and issue covered. The publication is sold with the idea that the publisher is not required to render accounting, officially permitted, or otherwise, qualified services. If advice is necessary, legal or professional, a practiced individual in the profession should be ordered.

- From a Declaration of Principles which was accepted and approved equally by a Committee of the American Bar Association and a Committee of Publishers and Associations.

In no way is it legal to reproduce, duplicate, or transmit any part of this document in either electronic means or in printed format. Recording of this publication is strictly prohibited and any storage of this document is not allowed unless with written permission from the publisher. All rights reserved.

The information provided herein is stated to be truthful and consistent, in that any liability, in terms of inattention or otherwise, by any usage or abuse of any policies, processes, or directions contained within is the solitary and utter responsibility of the recipient reader. Under no circumstances will any legal responsibility or blame be held against the publisher for any reparation, damages, or monetary loss due to the information herein, either directly or indirectly.

Respective authors own all copyrights not held by the publisher.
The trademarks that are used are without any consent, and the publication of the trademark is without permission or backing by the trademark owner. All trademarks and brands within this book are for clarifying purposes only and are the owned by the owners themselves, not affiliated with this document.

Table of Contents

Introduction 4
Chapter 1: Why is Self-Confidence Important? 10
Chapter 2: The Real Power of Self-Confidence 16
Chapter 3: Self-Esteem Vs Self-Confidence 21
Chapter 4: The Most Common Way to Build Self-Confidence 27
Chapter 5: Build on Your Self-Esteem to Boost Your Self-Confidence 32
Chapter 6: Figure Out Who You Are 38
Chapter 7: What Can You Be Passionate About? 51
Chapter 8: Fine-tune Your Passions to Build Self-Esteem 56
Chapter 9: What's Holding You Back? 64
Chapter 10: Project Your Celebration of Your Impact on Others . 72
Chapter 11: Project What You Want to See 79
Chapter 12: Allow Yourself to Celebrate Daily Wins 85
Chapter 13: Practice Affirmations on Two Levels 88
Chapter 14: Kill the Negative Self-Talk 94
Chapter 15: Turn Self-Confidence into a Habit 98
Chapter 16: Put Together Your 30 Day Self-Confidence Building Plan 101
Conclusion 103

Introduction

This book is NOT theory. It's not a mishmash of scientific studies aimed at helping solve your problem with the right theory-based "solutions". It's not a loose collection of speculation about methods and tips that may explain your situation, which may have worked for other people. This information is not offered in the hopes that somehow, someway it "might" work for you.

Instead, everything you would read in this book works because they are sourced directly from my life. I lived out every lesson I share in this book. Indeed, every insight, every nugget of knowledge and every revelation I share in this book is made possible only through my hard-won experience. Everything you read in this book I learned firsthand.

It wasn't an easy process. I definitely didn't seek out to write all these out from the beginning. I was just simply living my life. Still, because of the things that I've learned and the results that I have gotten, I feel compelled to write this book. If what I discovered helped me turn my life around, I am confident it can help you turn your life around as well.

I had a real tough time being confident for the first 26 years of my life. When I was 3, my parents left me in the care of my grandparents as my dad got a job at a Middle Eastern oil company. I didn't live with my parents again until I turned 11 years old. Those 8 years of missing my parents really hit me hard. Somehow, someway, I believed the reason they left me was because I did something wrong. I blamed myself. I walked around with a tremendous burden of guilt. I always automatically blame myself if anything wrong happened in my life.

Well, my parents came back to the US for good. It just wasn't the same; I thought I was living with strangers. We didn't see eye to eye. In fact, it got so rough that I even ran away a couple of times. To say that the relationship was strained and awkward is to put in mildly - very mildly. I harbored a low-grade yet burning resentment against my parents. Worst of all, I blamed myself.

Whenever something wrong happened in my life or whenever things didn't pan out like I hoped, I always blamed myself first. In fact, I would lay the blame on myself and refuse to think that other people or other situations may have contributed to the situation. It always came down to me. This self-blame and self-hate were instinctive. I kept telling myself, "You don't deserve to get picked for the basketball team because you suck," or "She didn't call you back because why would she want to hang out with a loser like you?" and so on and so forth.

I had this mental audiotape that I kept playing back and the theme was the same: I'm a loser, and I don't deserve anything. Even though I got good grades and finished college and grad school, all my accomplishments were bittersweet - I always doubted myself. When I got the top score in a grad school section (I beat out over 250 other people!) I said to myself that I just got lucky. I dismissed that accomplishment.

I had this amazing certificate hanging on my wall, which is quite rare. Very few people have that accomplishment because very few people beat a class that size. The subject was very complicated and very difficult. Still, I dismissed it all as dumb luck. Maybe they were too hung over to study, maybe they were just too busy with other stuff.

I kept coming up with alternative reasons to rob myself of a sense of accomplishment and achievement. I kept sabotaging myself. I never allowed myself to celebrate my unique value as a person and my capacity to deliver happiness to others. I never celebrated my accomplishments. I settled for jobs that pay way less than what I was worth and what I was trained for. I hung out with people who took me for granted. I was perfectly happy to be at another totally forgettable "face in the crowd". I fell into relationships where I was neglected, overlooked, taken for granted, you name it.

Throughout it all, I had the attitude that I deserved exactly what life dished at me. It was, after all, the best I could expect since I wasn't worth much in my own eyes. Things could have continued this way had it not been for the fact that my almost non-existent self-esteem was corroding everything else in my life. It was this toxic factor that made everything else more bitter, painful, frustrating, and pointless. The more I believed that I was not worth anything, the more I struggled in all areas of my life. We're talking about my appearance, the jobs that I had, my career prospects, social status, even the size of the place I lived in and the kind of car I drove, everything was just poisoned by this, but I refused to see it.

My Relationships got Worse and Worse

Each and every new relationship led to worse and worse humiliations and compromises. I reached the point where I felt that if I were to stand up for myself, my significant other would automatically leave. There will be no discussion; she would just get up and out of my life. I felt that I have to hold everything in; I felt that whatever opinions I may have, whatever I feel I deserve, I have to hold it in because I don't want to turn anybody off. I could not afford that risk.

My jobs became daily humiliations. I mean, I expected to be the underdog - the guy at the bottom of the pile - but people at work were, to my face, reveling in the fact that I was the guy at the bottom. They would make a big deal out of it. They would point it out to my face that I was the guy at the bottom, and I wasn't going anywhere. This all happened despite the fact that I got better grades than these people. These all happened despite the fact that I went to a much better school than them. None of that mattered. All they knew was that I was the guy at the bottom, and they had the right to kick me when I'm down. The worst part to all of this is that I felt I deserved it. I felt that I could not do any better.

As I was drinking coffee alone at the company dining hall, it all came crashing down on me like a house of cards. I asked myself a very simple question; it turned out to be the key to me turning my life around. I asked myself, "Is this all life has to offer?" I was staring at the bottom of my empty coffee cup, and I could see the droplets of coffee slowly swirling around the coffee cup as I moved it. I kept asking myself that question as I stared at the nearly empty bottom of my cup.

There I was, giving the very best years of my life to a company that didn't even treat me like I existed-much less mattered. I was in relationships wracked with insecurity and co-dependency. I never had time to explore hobbies and interests that mattered to me. I felt like I was living my life for other people, trying to impress people that I didn't particularly like. I was wasting the majority of my time making sure everyone else was happy. Deep down inside, I was miserable. Deep down inside, I was crying, broken, dejected and alone. Enough is enough!

This book steps through the information I learned firsthand. As I struggled to put together a life for myself - based on my terms and my needs, in other words, a life worth living, it all boiled down to building my self-confidence.

Once I gained self-confidence, I've been able to turn my life around. It's completely black and white from how I used to live my life. Now, all my relationships are fulfilling and rewarding on so many levels. I'm surrounded only by people who respect me, and who value my worth. I am now doing work I find fulfilling, rewarding and personally important and meaningful. Each day is a day of discovery and victory. Best of all, I no longer view myself as the guy who's lucky to have crumbs at the end of the day.

I no longer view myself as the guy at the bottom of the pile who deserves to be there. Instead, I'm the guy who makes things happen in my life instead of the one who stands powerlessly by as life unfolds asking, "What happened?" In short, I went from a self-defined and self-sabotaging victim to a victor.

If you want to start living a life of victory, personal power, direction and meaning, the important lessons on self-confidence I have learned firsthand can benefit you. Why? Self-confidence is crucial to a life worth living. Even if you don't have big dreams for yourself, you still need confidence just to make sure you get what you deserve or what you have coming to you.

Self-confidence is crucial for identity; it ensures you a specific place in this world.

No one can give you self-confidence except yourself. It is a matter of personal realization.

Who is this Book for?

- People who struggle with self-esteem issues
- People who feel they're not living up to their fullest potential
- People who have a tough time making their dreams come true
- People who feel their voices are not being heard
- People who see the corrosive effects that low self-confidence has on their performance in all areas of their lives, as well as their impact on others

What will this book do for you?

You will get information you need to put together a personal framework that will help you become more effective in whatever situation you find yourself in. You will get information you need that can help you develop better self-esteem and improve your view of your personal worth. You will learn how to speak up for your rights and demand what is yours. You will learn to be a more effective person all around. You will learn to command the respect you deserve.

Benefit from my own experience. Read chapter 1 to begin your journey to a life of greater self-confidence, control and power over your life.

Chapter 1: Why is Self-Confidence Important?

Self-confidence is the fountainhead of everything else in your life. You draw from it to achieve and build the other areas of your life. Think of it as the fuel tank of your life. It's obviously not the physical fuel; it's not something that you can reduce to a substance, but nonetheless, it exists. People might not realize this but self-confidence gives you power to achieve in all areas of your life.

Career

Self-confidence is important for your career because, like it or not, businesses are looking for leaders. When you check out that want ad, and you see that they're looking for an entry-level person, you can bet that if you are a person who positions himself or herself as a future leader, you will go places in that company. It doesn't matter whether you applied for a seemingly dead-end job; once the business enterprise sees you as potential leader material, they would invest in you. They would have a vested interest in your personal development. You have to understand that businesses live or die based on how effectively they can turn rank and file employees into leaders.

Now, this leadership position can take a wide variety of shapes. You can be a frontline leader, meaning like you can be a low-level manager. You can be a member of the middle management, or you can become a vice-president or even CEO. It all really depends on you.

What's important to understand here is that businesses are desperate for future leaders because, let's face it, the vast majority of people who apply for jobs do so because they just need to pay the rent. They're just looking to making ends meet. They're not looking at the future; they're looking at their short-term needs and, accordingly, most of them never become leaders. It's completely outside of their conception of their place in the company. They're just looking to solve a problem.

If you're a confident person, you can become a leader. You can project an air that things can be done. You can inspire others, not only with your productivity, but with the emotional signals that you send out. People become optimistic around you. You can boost productivity simply because you inspire people.

These are the types of individuals businesses are looking to develop and promote, because if they are able to produce enough leaders, they will blow away their competition. Why? Their competition is staffed by people who have very short-term attitudes. Those people are simply looking to do a day's work for a day's pay. Nothing more, nothing less. A company staffed almost 100% of people with that mentality isn't going far. It will always be beaten by companies that have leaders. However, for you to become a leader, you have to have self-confidence.

Relationships

Relationships involve two different people, two different egos, two different backgrounds, and two different pasts. Whenever there is difference, it can be a very exciting thing because, let's face it, there's nothing more exciting than talking and dealing with somebody who experienced things that are very different from yours.

Now, as amazing as this difference may be, it also leads to conflict, because you didn't come from the same place. You didn't experience the same things; you didn't have the same ideas and influences growing up. Accordingly, when you're in a relationship, it's too easy to look at it as competition. It's too easy to look at it as somebody winning and somebody losing.

Unfortunately, if you have low self-confidence, it's very easy for you to gravitate towards an attitude where you believe that it's better not to assert yourself and your needs lest the other person might leave. In other words, you let your fear of losing them take over your relationship. It's no longer a relationship at that point.

You have to remember that relationships are spaces and arrangements that let both people grow. It's very hard to grow when you're always denying yourself. It's very hard to truly blossom when you feel like you have to hold yourself in because you're afraid that you would lose the other person in the relationship. Ultimately, without self-confidence your identity in the relationship becomes subsumed into the identity of your partner. In other words, the relationship is all about them, their needs, their plans, their future, and you then are left making all sorts of excuses as to why you let this happen.

One common excuse is to simply fool yourself into thinking that you're doing everything that you could do to support the relationship. You're not supporting the relationship because you're completely out of it. The relationship is not your partner. Unfortunately, that's when your support takes the form of denying yourself and your needs and your identity within the relationship. All you're managing to do is support your partner and nobody else.

You need to be strong in your conviction to keep on loving. You need to carve out your own identity. You need to make sure that your relationship is built on a solid foundation of respect and equality. None of these are possible if you don't have self-confidence.

For your relationship to be healthy, you have to get noticed. The other partner must not only notice you but give you proper respect and take your feedback. Furthermore, they must defer to you from time to time. In other words, you need to make your voice felt. This is almost impossible to do without self-confidence.

Another reason why self-confidence helps you in your relationship is because, let's face it, there's no such thing as a perfect relationship. People can and do screw up. Your partner or you can be unfaithful. You can say the wrong things at the wrong time and hurt each other. All sorts of things can go wrong.

Given all this, it's important to persevere. It's important to bounce back in a relationship. Make no mistake about it, your partner can say something so crushing, so cutting and so humiliating that it's very easy for you to throw in the towel and just walk out. However, you don't. If the relationship is worth it, you don't. You hang in there. It requires resilience. You need to hang in there long enough for you to communicate in such a way that he or she learns from that sad experience and gives you proper respect. That's not going to happen if you don't have enough self-confidence going in.

It's too easy for your relationship to become so fragile based on such low self-esteem that its only a matter of time until either of you walks away. If you think this is difficult enough, understand that getting into a relationship in the first place requires confidence. Why? You need to stand out from other suitors.

If your partner is very attractive or appealing, you can bet that there would be other suitors. It depends on their level of appeal. Of course, the more attractive or appealing the partner, the more competition you have. However, even if your partner is not all that attractive, there's still at least one person that is interested in your partner, or your partner might be interested in somebody else. To stand out from the competition, you need self-confidence. At the very least, you should be able to make a case for yourself as to why your prospective partner should pick you instead of somebody else.

Life Enjoyment

In terms of quality of life, self-confidence is crucial. Seriously, you can't live your life in the shadows. If you don't have self-confidence, you resign yourself to being yet another face in the crowd. You start believing that you really don't matter all that much. You start believing that you really can't speak up because your voice doesn't really count for anything.

You can't live life without speaking out for your needs. Why? People can and will step on you. You see, life is a dog-eat-dog landscape; it really is. Forget everything that you've heard before. It's not a world of sunshine, smiles, unicorns and lollipops. It can be brutal out there. Unfortunately, far too many people move in when they detect any kind of weakness. If you give somebody an inch, it's not uncommon for them to want to take a mile. If you give somebody a hand, don't be surprised if they want to take your arm as well.

You have to be able to speak up for your needs. You have to be able to stand on your rights. You can't just live in the shadows and constantly give in. It's going to get in the way of your enjoyment of your life. You feel you're simply settling for something that is getting smaller and smaller with each passing day. You start feeling that you are a bystander in your life, and regardless of how you feel, and regardless of what's going on, and how hurt you become, it really doesn't really matter all that much because you don't matter all that much. You see how corrosive this is? You understand how you have set up yourself to live such a pathetic life? It is pathetic because you are capable of so much more.

The bottom line is if you want to be successful in anything, you have to be confident in yourself. Nobody can do it for you. Nobody else would do it for you. Nobody else can do it for you.

Chapter 2: The Real Power of Self-Confidence

Let me clue you in on a secret. This is a secret because a lot of people don't like to admit this. The secret is most people are unsure; most people lack confidence. Now, don't get too excited. Lacking confidence does not necessarily mean that they have absolutely no self-confidence. They lack enough confidence. In other words, it's below the level that they need to live their lives at peak performance.

Now, this revelation is actually quite apparent. You just examine all the lives of people you know, and I can guarantee you that 80% of the time, they are living below their fullest potential. In other words, they are capable of so much more yet they settle for a life that is several levels below that full potential. They're settling; they're taking second place. They're not venturing forth to the fullest extent of what they are capable of getting out of life.

Again, the reason for this is that they lack confidence. They are not confident enough. This is why people who possess self-confidence at high levels are very magnetic. People who lack confidence are drawn to confident people. Now, don't get too excited. It's easy to see the positive aspect of this; it's very easy to see people who are drawn to you, and they encourage you. The bottom line, whether they say it or not, is that I'm drawn to you because you have something that I don't have at a high enough level.

However, you can also draw people in the wrong ways. There are people who lack confidence, and they know it, so they try to attack, expose, or put on the spot people who are obviously more confident than them. There is always that variation.

The bottom line is that in whatever form it takes, confident people are "magnetic" precisely because they make people around them feel comfortable. Again, there is negative magnetism because people who are envious of what you have. They want to be comfortable, but they feel they have to attack you because they feel that's the only way they can make up for their own lack of confidence.

Regardless, when you're confident, you're automatically magnetic. Confident people fulfill other people's perception or wish for comfort and support. In other words, people around you are looking for leadership. They're like lost sheep looking for a shepherd. I know that sounds insulting because when you say to someone's face that he is acting like a sheep, don't be surprised if you get a fist in your mouth.

But that's the truth, people at some level or another, lack enough confidence, and they know this. This is why they naturally gravitate towards people with a healthy level of easily visible and easily detected self-confidence. Why does this happen? Why are people looking for leadership? Well, confident people make those around them feel things are possible. This is the mark of leadership. When you make people around you feel that certain things are possible, they can't get enough of you. Why? Left to their own devices or left to themselves, they feel things are harder than they really are. They feel that things are not easy and that there are many obstacles along the way.

When you come around and inspire them, and they feel that things are possible, they can't help but sit up and pay attention. You make them feel the certain things that they can't normally feel on their own. If you hang around long enough confident people, they get others to feel that things are not only possible, but probable. This is what people are looking for in leadership. This is what people are looking for in their social circles.

Have you ever noticed groups of teenagers and that some of them are more aggressive than others? Well, when you take a group of teenage boys, who are otherwise usually timid, and throw in there a leader of the same age who motivates them to do certain things, you'd be surprised as to what that group can do. Of course, this can play out either positively or negatively.

A lot of the hooligan violence and gang violence that you hear about in the news usually involve groups of teenagers that have a leader or two that push them to feel that certain things are not only possible, but probable. Rob a liquor store? Well, if the leader is not in the mix, then that's just an idle fantasy. Once you throw in the right person in their midst, it's only a matter of time until the group knocks over a liquor store.

You see how this works? This can play out positively or negatively. But the truth cannot be denied that confident people get others around them to feel that things are not only possible but probable. I don't know about you, but that is the definition of power.

The Bottom Line

Confident people can create a "personal reality field" around themselves. It's easy for you to walk around and think that certain things are possible, and certain things are not possible. Everybody is entitled to that. However, the moment you come across somebody who is very confident, it's very easy for you to fall under their influence. It's very easy for you to believe that they're persuasive.

Now, their answers to the questions you're confronting may not be all that better than your answers, but it wouldn't feel like it. Why? Their level of self-confidence is so infectious that it persuades you to think that if this person seems so gung-ho about what they're saying, it must be true. You might be absolutely correct in your conclusion because you're thinking might be based on logic and reason and past experiences, but all of that goes out the window. Instead, you're just blown away by this person's confidence, and you allow that factor to persuade you to come to an opposite conclusion.

Confident people also create a personal reality field around them through group cohesion. Believe it or not, when two or more people hang out in the same group, and they start repeating certain things, they start hypnotizing each other. They start persuading each other to think that ideas that they individually have a problem with are true. There is such a thing as group thinks, and the cause of such group cohesion is, you guessed it, confident people.

Once this happens, confident people can marshal the individual strengths and competencies of the group towards common goals. This is the essence of leadership. What's important to understand here is that just because you're able to do this because of your natural confidence, it doesn't automatically mean that you will have formal leadership roles, at least in the beginning. In other words, just because you are able to do this, don't think that your boss will automatically say, "Okay, you're promoted." It sometimes takes a while; there is such a thing as office politics after all.

However, the place that you work for would be stupid to overlook your organic leadership because whether people have fancy titles or occupy high places in the hierarchy chart, their natural leadership isn't undeniable. It really is the organization's loss to continue to turn a blind eye to the organic leadership of certain individuals in the organization. I need you to keep this in mind because it's easy to think of self-confidence as something that would be "nice to have." No, it's not an option.

If you want to go anywhere in life, if you want to live up to your fullest potential, if you want to stop living a life of frustration and disappointment, you need to invest time, effort and energy in building up your self-confidence, and it will turn you into an organic leader who will, sooner or later, turn into a formal leadership role.

Chapter 3: Self-Esteem Vs Self-Confidence

A lot of people confuse self-esteem and self-confidence. In fact, when a lot of people talk about self-confidence, they're actually talking about self-esteem and vice versa. It's too easy for a lot of people to think that self-esteem and self-confidence are one and the same. No, they're not. They're two totally different things. They do impact yourself; that's one thing they have in common. But in the way they operate and their impact, as well as application, they run on completely different tracks.

In this chapter, I'm going to separate the two so you can have a clear idea of what self-esteem and what self-confidence is. The reason why I need to separate the two is because we're trying to solve a problem. You are suffering from low self-confidence; we're trying to fix that problem. Unfortunately, it's hard to fix a problem if you don't define it properly. If you think that a problem is A and then you define it as B, even the best solutions for B are not going to make the problem of A go away. I hope that much is clear.

It is really important to understand how self-esteem and self-confidence are different from each other while also being related to each other. By knowing how these two concepts play out in your life, you can then put together a winning framework that would enable you to live life with greater self-confidence. That is our ultimate goal. But to get there, we still need to address self-esteem.

What is Self-Esteem?

Self-esteem is your valuation of yourself. You look at yourself, and you come up with all sorts of judgments. You come up with this story or personal narrative of your value as a person, your place in the world and your worth. Are you worth sacrificing for? Are you worth much of anything? How important are you? These are questions of self-esteem. These are value questions and you yourself put value on yourself.

What is self-confidence? Self-confidence is the external projection of the value, place, worth, importance and effectiveness you feel. While self-esteem is completely internal, meaning this plays out in an internal dialogue and personal narrative that few people could see, self-confidence is very much public.

Let's put it this way, if you think you are a complete failure, then you'd start acting like a person who is prone to fail. You start acting like a person who doesn't have much value, someone who doesn't respect himself or herself.

Self-confidence is all about the signals you send to the rest of the world as to how it should interpret you and value you. As you could probably already tell, self-confidence and self-esteem are joined at the hip; they flow from the same place. While one is purely internal, the other is external and public. This is what leads to confusion. A lot of people think that they're one and the same. They do come from the same place, but self-esteem is purely internal.

Now, let's put it this way, people might think you're a success. People might think that you're rich, powerful and amazing. These are all external judgments. However, if you think that you are worthless and a pile of trash, no external validation is ever going to make your self-esteem issues go away. Self-esteem, after all, is inner valuation of your worth, and it fits a personal narrative about your value, your place in the world, your worth and your importance.

Self-Esteem is Internal Self-Confidence

I don't want to confuse you, but if you're looking for a simple summation of self-esteem, it's this: it's internalized self-confidence. Basically, you look at your value as a person, and you believe that you have value. You can do it. You do have what it takes, you do belong, and so on and so forth. It's really just an internalization of your capacity, and the value that you choose for yourself.

However, it's important to note that self-esteem all goes back to inner valuation. It's all inner; it's internalized. You focus on your value, and you focus on what's your worth.

The External Components of Self-Confidence

If self-esteem is internalized self-confidence, then self-confidence is externalized self-esteem. Now, I don't want to confuse you here but since the base of your personality is what you choose to value yourself, meaning your self-esteem, then it follows that what you do as far as the world is concerned is an emanation or an outward working of what's going on inside. In other words, it begins with your self-esteem and what you choose to believe about yourself. It begins with your personal narrative regarding your place in the world, your value, your importance and what you're capable of. However, it progresses from there and works itself out.

What is the objective manifestation of this? What does the world see? Well, the world outside would pick up certain clues. It would pay attention to your body language. Do you carry yourself in a way that people feel that you are confident about your ability to get things done? Or at the very least, confident that you know what you're talking about? Does your body language reflect this?

People would also pay attention to your facial expressions. Do you have a tough time looking people in the eye? Do you always feel that you have to look sideways because you are embarrassed? Do you have a tough time giving certain expressions? These are also interpreted because confident people have certain facial expressions. They're not out to dominate other people; they're not out to hit people over the head with their confidence. Instead, their confidence is easy. It puts people at ease but at the same time, you can tell that this person is solid inside.

Furthermore, self-confidence is made manifest in how we handle situations. When something embarrassing happens, or can potentially lead to conflict, is it your instinct to immediately run away or say sorry? Does your instinct immediately take fault and just paper things over, and hope people would not see your screw-up? How you handle situations has an impact on how people would take you seriously.

If you're the type of person who is a take-charge type of person, people would sit up and pay attention, because there are few people like that. Most people are passive. How you handle situations is directly impacted by your level of self-confidence.

Even the words you choose are reflections of how confident you are. Confident people don't say, "I don't have any money. It's impossible." Instead, they use different phrasing. They say, "how can I do that? How can I raise the money?" In other words, they pose themselves a question that at least can have some sort of answer that would lead to their desired reality coming to pass.

Compare this with dismissive statements, saying, "I don't have the money. I'm broke. It's just not going to happen." Which type of person would you rather hang out with? I thought so.

Finally, another external component of self-confidence involves how you speak. If you're the type of person who can't speak with enough volume as to instill confidence regarding your competence, that's going to be an issue. People are not going to come to you for answers. People are not going to come to you to be inspired. How can you give them what they're looking for when it's obvious you don't even know what you're talking about? Or at least, you don't give out signals that you feel that what you're saying and what you believe are right?

How important are these external signals of self-confidence? Well, they're extremely important because they impact others to produce. Remember, when you are self-confident, you're not just self-confident because you have nothing else better to do. Self-confidence isn't just some sort of tag or label or some sort of decorative element. It's not like some sort of bright jacket you wear and that people would point out and say, "Oh. That's nice." No, it actually has an effect on people around you. When that effect happens, it then builds up to change your role.

Just how does this play out? Well, when you send out external signals of confidence, you impact other people to produce trust. They become more comfortable; they feel more familiar. They are more willing to help; all these lead to greater and greater levels of respect. All these also lead them to think that you're part of their team, that they're part of your team, that there's a connection between you.

In other words, when you are confident, you are able to change your surroundings and change your immediate reality for the better. That's how important self-confidence is, because let me tell you, the world couldn't care less about your feelings. Seriously, you can feel very powerful, but if it's internal, and it doesn't manifest itself into actions. You're just wasting your time, because the world only cares about the things that you do.

One way you "do things" is when you impact people enough or inspire them enough to do things for you or behave differently. You see how this works? That's how the world judges people. That's how the world sizes people up. It's all objective; it's all about results. All this talk about feelings, emotions, what could've happened, what should have happened or what they have intended, all that is rubbish.

At the end of the day, none of that really matters. All that matters as far as the world goes is what did you actually do? How did you change your surroundings? How much of an impact did you have on people around you? Did people stop behaving differently? In other words, the world looks at human relationships and human dynamics in terms of chain reactions that manifest themselves in actions. In other words, this is concrete. This is not theoretical; this is not speculation. Either you did something, or you didn't. You either had an impact or you didn't.

That's how important self-confidence is because on an objective level, it changes your reality. When you have an impact on others, they can behave differently, and you can start moving towards a common goal. You can start communicating with each other in a way that can make certain changes happen. Now, keep in mind that these changes can be positive or negative. That's not really the point. The point is the world only looks at you based on the results that you produce. This can be positive results, as well as negative results.

Chapter 4: The Most Common Way to Build Self-Confidence

Before we jump in with both feet, let me just make one thing clear. What will follow is information that would help you build a personal framework for boosting your self-confidence. I cannot emphasize the concept of 'personal framework' enough. This personal framework is simply scaffolding or a structure for your own efforts in building up your self-confidence. In other words, you have to fill in this framework with specific information from your life. Only you know that.

By giving you these broad guidelines, you can then fill in the details based on your set of circumstances, your experiences and your preferences. You have to steer clear of one-size-fits-all or magic bullet-type confidence-building 'solutions'. Most of them are not solutions at all because what works for one person may not work for you, and that is why it is much better to work with a framework. You can see enough details in the framework to remind you of certain things that are happening in your life. You can subsequently fit in personal details and then modify them as you implement the framework.

The secret to the framework is to implement it consistently. With constant practice, you can then zero in on the things that are working and later modify the things that are not. With enough implementation and ample time, you would have a framework that is finally tuned to your life. Not mine, not somebody else's, but your life. This is the key to success.

Again, steer clear of 'magic' checklists for building confidence. They almost always fail because they are based on somebody else's life. Those people do have different experiences than you. Those people may be facing dissimilar circumstances than you.

How can their solution, when taken on a point-by-point basis and applied wholesale work for you? It is simply not going to happen. It is trying to fit a square peg in a round hole.

Instead, use the framework and customize it based on your life. I just want to make this clear because it is too easy to look for 'magic' solutions that as long as you use these steps or tips, everything turns out awesome. They rarely do. You have to get in there and put in the work. You have to customize. You have to personalize the solutions so they speak to your particular set of circumstances. Otherwise, you would be settling for cents on the dollars so to speak at best, and completely failing at worst. With that said, let us begin.

The most common way to build self-confidence is just to go out there and project confidence. This is what a lot of other books say that you should do. You should simply go out there and just project confidence. You just look at confident people, try to read them, and then send out the same signals. What this really all boils down to is fake it until you make it. You know that it is fake because, deep down inside, you feel inadequate. Deep down inside, you feel like you are not worth much of anything, but you act like you are on top of the world. You act like you can get things done, and you have a deep and abiding faith in yourself.

The advantage of 'fake it until you make it' should be obvious. It is quick. It is fairly easy to implement. At your workplace, there is bound to be at least one confident person. You only need to look at that person, study them from afar and then start mirroring some of the things that they say, the things they do and their body language as well as appearance. Faking it until you make it almost takes no preparation. You can do it at the spur of the moment. You can feel inspired by a memory of a confident person who you met in school or at a previous job. You then channel that person into your social interactions in the here and now. It is a very free-form way of projecting confidence.

The big disadvantage of faking it until you make it is that it involves trial and error. As I have mentioned above, what works for somebody may not work for you. They may be giving off certain signals and pull it off perfectly. They are the masters of that kind of confidence; however, when you do it, you might actually fall flat on your face. You might truly make a bigger fool out of yourself.

Unfortunately, when you do things on a trial-and-error basis, when you commit an error, the emotional wounds might take a long time to heal. It is too easy to get traumatized when you screw because you are just faking it until you make it. Ultimately, you might crash and burn so hard that it would become very easy for you to develop unhealthy coping mechanisms to deal with judgment. You can become really shy; you can become very judgmental. You can adopt an attitude of ?'the best defense is a good offense'. In other words, you try to cover up your lack of self-confidence by simply being an offensive or cocky person. I am sure it is obvious to you how these coping mechanisms create more problems than they solve.

Buy Your Confidence

Another common way to build self-confidence is simply to buy it. I am not talking about buying confidence in the form of a pill or a capsule. I am definitely not talking about buying confidence in the form of some sort of Iron Man-like machine that encapsulates you in this amazing veneer of self-confidence. Instead, I am talking about buying trinkets, gadgets or possessions that make you feel more confident. The global fashion industry is in business partly because of this dynamic. A lot of people who have low self-esteem or who have low self-confidence would buy clothes to make themselves feel good or at least make themselves feel important. They fall into the old thinking of 'clothes make the man'. A lot of people also continue to believe that if you want to make a million bucks, you better dress like a million bucks.

In other words, it is the external trappings of your appearance are what reorganize the internal reality of your existence. As we will discuss later, this has it completely in reverse. It is actually the other way around. If you want to be confident, you have to start from the inside and work outwards. You have to start from the bedrock of yourself identity and work your way out. That is how you build on a solid foundation. However, if you build from outside perception courtesy of toys, gadgets and trinkets you buy, you are depending on your external casing to change you internally. The big advantage of buying your confidence is, first of all, it is quick and easy. If you have a credit card, or if you have a job, you can buy certain small trinkets and gadgets to buy yourself some respect. Now, keep in mind you are not really buying respect. You only think you are buying respect. You are just reading a lot of these positive meanings into people's reactions.

What you are really doing is you are just tapping into people's mental laziness. They take a symbol, and they project all sorts of meaning onto it. For example, if you were to roll into the parking lot in a brand-new Ferrari, people would look at your car and then look at you and make all sorts of instant connections. Since it is fairly rare for somebody to drive a car worth several hundred thousand dollars, it is very easy for people to jump into the conclusion that you are a winner, that you have made it, that you are a top dog and that you are a leader.

As you can well imagine, it may simply turn out that you borrowed your friend's Ferrari. It may turn out that you are a mechanic working on that Ferrari and just driving it around to test it. However, people are mentally lazy. They automatically take a symbol and project all sorts of meaning usually drawing from their own lack of self-confidence. Still, this way of projecting self-confidence is quick and easy.

Now, this method has a serious downside. First of all, it costs money. The more the self-confidence that you want to project, the more money it would take. For example, if you invite your buddies from high school for beer at your place, and they show up at a mansion, buying that mansion obviously can set you back quite a bit. Second, you are putting on a show. You are living for other people's expectations. In other words, your pay-off is the fact that they are reading meaning into what you are doing. It has nothing to do with what you have built for yourself and on your own.

If this is not bad enough, you have to put up with appearances. You have to understand that people give respect grudgingly, and for a lot of people, nothing would make them feel happier than to see others who they feel are superior to them slip up and fall. This, of course, leads to a tremendous amount of stress.

Moreover, deep down inside, you feel like a fraud or impostor. You feel like since you bought the external trappings of self-confidence that it is just a matter of time until people find you out. This is a tremendous amount of stress. This can be very, very tough on your nerves. Unfortunately, you bring this onto yourself when you feel that your trinkets, material possessions and other outward trappings ultimately define you. This is going to be a problem if you cannot keep up the expense of putting up appearances. Your self-respect as well as self-confidence goes down the tubes as others view of you changes due to your reversal in fortune.

Chapter 5: Build on Your Self-Esteem to Boost Your Self-Confidence

The methods discussed in Chapter 4 should be obviously problematic to you. If you read through the descriptions of those coping mechanisms and strategies for building self-confidence, it should become quickly apparent that they have serious limitations. While I am not going to pretend that those techniques work for some people, the truth is for the large majority of people trying them out, they often lead to disasters. They do not pan out and work out as expected.

Thankfully, there is a better alternative. The alternative is to work on your self-esteem. In other words, you need to work on transforming your self-confidence from the inside out. By building a solid foundation of self-worth and self-respect internally, you then project this outwards to greater and greater level of self-confidence. Is this going to happen overnight? Absolutely not. Is this easy? Well, for some people it is easier than for others, but it still requires effort. It, nonetheless, requires a certain degree of consistency and constant effort.

Unfortunately, the reason why buying your self-confidence or faking it until you make it are so popular with a lot of people is because they are simple to implement. When you buy a BMW or a Ferrari is relatively easy compared to working on your inner insecurities and a sense of inadequacy to build lasting self-confidence.

However, let me tell you, if you were to work from inside out, the results that you get would be more long-lasting. Additionally, you do not have to worry about being discovered as a fraud. You do not have to carry around constantly this guilt or worry because you feel somehow some way you are an impostor. With that said, at least understand that any internal-based solution will require some work. It will require some attention to detail. It will require consistency of action. If you are willing to commit to doing what is needed, then tremendous progress is possible for you.

How Does This Work?

Well, to build your self-confidence through boosting your self-esteem, you, first of all, change your self-perception. You change how you look at yourself and how you view yourself. Everybody has self-perception. We all have this mental picture in our minds of who we are, what we are capable of, and where we are going. We also have a picture of where we are in the greater scheme of things. In other words, we have a sense of place for ourselves. People who suffer from a low self-confidence obviously have negative views of these things. They feel that their place is at the bottom. They feel that they are not worth much of anything. They feel that whatever they try, mediocrity will result. The bottom line is they do not feel that they are anybody special.

You have to work on your self-perception. You have to change how you perceive yourself. You have to go from looking at yourself as this perpetual victim of situations and circumstances beyond your control to somebody who actually makes things happen. This is a tremendous leap in self-perception. You go from somebody who only sits passively and watches his or her life play out in front of him or her, to somebody who envisions themselves as a person who actually has a direct role in what is happening. Again, you go from a person who just stands back and looks in frustration at what happened to your life and constantly asking yourself what happened to the person who makes things happen.

All of this can be traced to self-perception. How do you picture yourself? How do you view yourself? What kind of mental picture do you have of yourself? This self-perception is crucial to self-definition. When you define yourself, you define what your limits are. You define what you are capable of. You define what holds you back or what pushes you forward. The best part to all of this is that you are always in control because you are the one doing the defining, not somebody else.

Changing Your Personal Narrative

Another key aspect of working on your self-esteem to boost your self-confidence is the fact that at some point you would have to change your personal narrative. As mentioned previously in this book, your personal narrative is really an ongoing story that you run in your mind. This is the organizing principle or organizing story that you subscribe to. All you experiences, all your interactions with the outside world and its people are filtered through this narrative.

For example, you have a narrative that you are an unwanted person, when you walk into the door and people look at you with a certain look in their faces; it is highly likely you would interpret that as a negative look. You would interpret the way they look at you as basically saying you should keep out. You are not wanted here. Go away!

If your personal narrative is that you are a valuable person and that people would be happy to have you around because you have something positive to contribute, you probably interpret that same look as an invitation to introduce yourself. Maybe you could look at it as a challenge to make a favorable impression. Whatever the case may be; you end up in a totally different place. Instead of feeling small, unwanted, shut out, rejected and frustrated, you can look at it as a neutral invitation for contact. You might even look at it as a positive opportunity. Do you see how important your personal narrative is?

Your personal narrative is crucial to how you interpret your reality because, believe it or not, all the things that we take as objective truth are actually judgments. That is all they are. Two people can look at the same set of facts and walk away two totally different interpretations. Their personal narratives determine the difference in these interpretations. When you work on building up on your self-confidence through working on your self-esteem, you necessarily have to swap out your personal narrative. There has to be certain changes in your personal narrative for this inside-out process to work.

Change Your Mental Patterns

The funny thing about people's perception of reality is that, in many cases, their perception of reality is really just a product of their mental habits. If you habitually interpret things, in the worst way possible, it is very easy for you to conclude that this is the only way people can interpret these signals. This is the only judgment they can have. After all, since you automatically conclude things are a certain way when you get particular feedback or specific stimuli, then that must be reality. Well, it may turn out that you think that way accordingly because it is your mental habit. Your mental patterns are set up in such a way that you always end up with a certain conclusion.

What if you were to change your mental habits? What if you were to modify your mental patterns? Does it necessarily mean that you would end up with the same judgments? Chances are very high that you might actually have a different view of your self-worth and personal value once your mental habits change.

Now, the key fact to take away here is that mental habits are chosen. I know that sounds crazy because you might be thinking: Well, I was simply born this way. This is just how I think. You might want to think again because the way you interpret your reality had to come from somewhere. It is something that you picked up or learned along the way. Most of us learn our mental habits from our parents. We also learn it from the people we hang out with consistently. There is such a thing as group think. If you change your group of friends, you would be surprised as to how your mental habits and attitude change.

Regardless, you need to question your mental habits. It is something you choose. It is not something that you are born with. It is not something that is imposed on you and that you have no choice over. You always have a power of choice. You can always to be conscious of your mental habits and buck against it.

Once Your Self-Esteem is Positive, You Project It Out

After you have gone through the process of changing your self-perception, swapping out or modifying your personal narrative, and identifying, disrupting and replacing your mental patterns, the next step is to project it out. In other words, you go from the internal to the external. You go from emotions to intentions to actions. As I have mentioned previously, the world does not care about your feelings. It does not care about the inner turmoil you are going through unless it has an external effect. The world is purely external. All it cares about is the things that you actually do.

You can think of all sorts of murderous things. You can think of all sorts of screwed up, messed up, tragic things, but unless you act on them or, at the very least, verbalize them, the world does not care. Do you see how this works? So, for your self-esteem to truly boost your self-confidence, you need to project it out. You need to act on it. It has to have an impact on how you actually behave.

The good news is that this does not have to be super-dramatic. You do not have to necessarily live out a Hollywood movie of somebody who was a bookworm and who is unsure of himself suddenly blossoming into this super-confident person who gets members of the opposite sex, gets promoted, and becomes master of his or her world. It does not have to be that way. We, after all, do not live in Hollywood. Any small changes that you detect can be scaled up.

Also, this does not have to happen overnight. You have to understand that your mental patterns are mental patterns precisely because they are habits. As you probably already know, habits are hard to break. We are creatures of comfort. Once we get set in our ways, it is very hard for us to change. We fear change. Still, if you are focused on changing your mental habits because you have changed your self-perception as well as your personal narrative, progress is possible. However, it will not happen overnight. It will not be easy. It will not be quick.

The best news here is that when you work from the inside out, you are starting with something real. You are also starting with something substantive. You are building from the building blocks of your personality which is your self-perception, personal narrative and mental patterns. Once you have modified these; then project out, and the world responds accordingly. As soon as the world responds to your altered behavior that is when you know this change has become real.

Otherwise, as far as the world is concerned, this is all internal. It is all about your feelings and as I keep repeating, the world does not care about your feelings. It could not care less. For this to become real, you have to let it change how you actually behave. That is how your increased self-confidence will have an impact on your world.

Chapter 6: Figure Out Who You Are

The first step in changing yourself internally so you can have greater self-confidence is to do a self-assessment. Who are you? You might be saying I know who I am. I am the same person I was 10 years ago. Well, think again. You have to get real. Unfortunately, a lot of people who are suffering from low self-esteem blow things up out of proportion. They think that they are worse than they actually are. They think that they are weaker than they truly are. They think they are insignificant.

You have to get real. You cannot engage in denial. You also cannot engage in self-delusion. This is another trap that too many people fall into. One common delusion is that you are powerless in your world. Regardless what you do, regardless of what you try, nothing will really change.

Well, the fact that you have so much power over what you choose to believe about yourself highlights the amount of power you have. Can you imagine if you chose to do things differently? Can you imagine if you chose to see yourself differently? So, it is really important to get out from under any type of self-delusion or exaggeration.

Furthermore, you have to stop blaming other people. Stop blaming people who may have hurt you in the past. Stop blaming people who may have traumatized you. Sure, they did bad things to you, but it is still your choice in the here and now to let those bad experiences have a negative effect on you now. What matters is today. The past is the past. Unless you have access to a time machine, you really cannot do anything about what happened in the past. The worst thing that you can do as far as your personal power is concerned is to let the past constantly affect your future. Do you think remembering how embarrassed and humiliated you felt because people made fun of you will empower you today? No, it will not, not in a million years.

Instead, you will just work to torpedo whatever self-confidence you have built today. It is like picking on a scab. Your wound already healed; however, when you pick on the scab, there is a new wound. It then heals, and afterward crusts over. You then pick it again, and there is a new wound. You have to let the past go and stop blaming it for who you have become today. You have to let go of your tendency to blame. All of us are not immune to this. All of us, at some level or other, like to blame others because, hey it feels great. It lets us off the hook.

However, the problem is the more we blame others for our failings; the harder it is for us to actually take power over our lives. If you think about it, the more you blame another person, the greater power you give them. Why? Deep down inside, you are programming yourself to believe that if this person is to blame for my problems, then this person has caused my problems.

Now, logically speaking, if there is a cause, then the cause is also the solution to your problem. In other words, that person in your past is the only one who can fix the damage that they caused. Now, I am sure you do not need me to remind you of how impossible this is. You cannot control that person. In fact, that person has probably moved on, is very happy with his or her life and could not care less about your situation. In reality, that person very likely even forgot about you. Now, here you are constantly blaming that person, but the only thing you are achieving is reminding yourself it is only that person who can fix your problem.

The solution here is simple. Stop blaming. That way, the ability to fix your situation comes back to you. You always have a choice on how you respond to memories, to present situations and to worries about the future. It is your ability to choose the proper response that can either give you power or take it away. Blaming is never a winning strategy because you hand off power to people, situations and circumstances you have no control over.

Similarly, justifications do not work. When you justify why you have such low self-confidence, you are not doing yourself any favors. You are basically just giving yourself permission to continue what you are doing. You are merely giving yourself permission to not solving your problems. Justifications are cop-outs. They are just excuses you made for yourself not to try. They are just excuses for yourself to remain a coward.

It takes courage to want to change. It takes courage to own up to certain facts about your life. You need to go through these very important questions and realizations for you to truly answer the question: Who am I? Otherwise, you will end up in a haze. It would be all foggy for you because there are all sorts of blame, excuses, justifications and denial. It is going to be very hard in that haze to tell what is real and what is an illusion.

Who Are You Really? Right Here, Right Now

You have to ask yourself what your identity is in the here and now. It is really important to zero in on who you truly are. We are not talking about who you would like yourself to be in the future. We are not talking about who you thought you were in the past. We are talking about who you are right now and right here.

This is very tricky because this question inevitably slams into another question. Most people think they are somebody else. This question slams into the other question of who you think you are. Now, this might seem like some sort of philosophical empty talk. This might seem like some kind of theoretical psychoanalysis, but this is real because the answer to your question is actually simpler than you think.

You can quickly weed out who you think you are, meaning your internal idealized picture of yourself versus who you really are. How? Look at your behavior. That is the real test. When you look at how you behave, you can quickly compare it with who you think you are.

A lot of people who are suffering from low self-confidence think they are a victim. They think that they are the guy at the bottom. They think that they are the person who is constantly being picked on. Now, when they compare that with their actual behavior, it might not be as bad as you think.

Similarly, you might think that you are doing well enough, and that you are in the middle of the bell curve, so to speak, in terms of self-confidence. However, if you stack that up against your true behavior, it may indeed turn out that you actually have very, very low self-confidence or even non-existent self-confidence. How does this work? Well, it is simple. Again, it is all about objective reality. We are all entitled to think what we want about ourselves in our reality.

However, what really matters is how we behave, because our behavior and action set our material reality. That is what the world pays attention to. Those kind of external signals are what change our immediate surroundings. It is important to always go back to the objective standard of actual behavior. When you look at your behavior, then you can answer the following questions: What limitations do you have? What makes you wait?

People who suffer from low self-confidence feel that there are certain limitations holding them back and keeping them down. They feel that there are definite boundaries that they cannot cross. They feel that there are certain things that they simply cannot do. Regardless of how hard they try; regardless of how much they want to do it; they just cannot do it. These are, of course, mental limitations.

In addition, it is important to pay attention to the tendency to wait. A lot of people spend their lives waiting for things to pan out in their lives. It is like they are waiting for some cosmic signal from the universe for them to take action; then and only then would they do whatever it takes for however long it takes to succeed. However, until that happens, they are just perfectly content to wait.

I hope you can see what is wrong with this picture because unless you have a healthy self-esteem, it is too easy for you to content yourself with waiting. You are waiting for things to 'feel right'. You are waiting for the 'right people' to show up in your life. You are waiting for the universe to send you the precise signals for you to make the hard decisions that would turn your life around. In other words, you are waiting for all of these to finally start acting confident.

Well, I have some bad news for you. If you are waiting for other people and circumstances and situations, you are waiting for things that are outside your control. The chances of you waiting forever are quite high. So, stop waiting for the world. Stop waiting for those magic signals that the world would send you. The world has enough problems of its own. It turns on its axis. It has its own agenda. In other words, the world has its own life.

You have to take action now. You have to take initiative. You cannot trick yourself into kicking the can down the road as far as self-confidence goes because you were waiting for some sort of signal.

Comparative Approaches to Determining Your Identity

The previous section in this chapter dealt with proactive steps you could take to determine who you are. If that is too hard, or it does not really line up with your personal preferences, you can try a comparative approach. Compare yourself to others to see who you are by identifying what you are not. Just as we can tell what a square is by putting it side by side with a circle or a triangle, compare your personality with other people you know. The more different you are from these people, the clearer your identity becomes. Again, you should pay attention to behavior. Behavior does not lie. When you focus on your intentions and other internal factors, it is too easy to become delusional.

Compare yourself to people you know who are positive, confident and doing well in life. How do you stack up? Now, please understand that your low self-esteem is probably going to blow things out of proportion. For example, a woman who is slightly prettier than you might seem like a goddess compared to you because of your low self-esteem. Regardless, these differences are instructive. You just have to factor in the fact that your low self-esteem tends to blow things up out of proportion.

Once you have done that, the next step is to compare yourself to people you do not want to become. This method of comparative identity really turns on cautionary tales. In other words, when you compare your life, to somebody you know who you do not want to become, you look at their lives as cautionary tales. You look at their lives as a series of decisions that you do not want to make because you know where it leads.

Why is this important? Why are cautionary tales valuable? Well, when you look at the cautionary tales posed by other people's life histories and experiences, you get a clear understanding of what your values are. You get an absolute understanding of what kind of character you would like to have. Again, there really is no right or wrong answer here. Instead, you are using cautionary tales as a spotlight to tell you certain key information about yourself.

For example, if somebody's life projects cautionary tales regarding bad investments, bad financial decisions, this tells you that you value money. You also value making the right decisions to make certain things happen in the future. Use these cautionary tales to give your composite view of your character and your value system.

Figure Out Who You Are Through Your Aspirations

The next step in this detective story of clearly identifying who you are involves your aspirations. You have to ask yourself what kind of life would I be living if I had all the confidence in the world? This is really important because you take your eyes off your limitations, and you focus on what you can work with in an ideal setting. You would be surprised as to what you would find out. This is actually pretty straightforward. You take who you are right now or whatever you know about yourself right now and just add supreme confidence.

Just assume that you wake up tomorrow, and you are the most confident person on the planet. Now ask yourself what would be different? How would you feel? How would you act? What kind of impact would you have on people around you?

Self-Assessment Exercise

To clarify things and make this chapter as practical as possible, I need you to answer the following questions. Whip out a piece of paper and write down the statement ?'I am _____'. In the underline section, type in all the adjectives that you think describe you. This has to be both positive and negative. None of us are 100% demons nor are we 100% angels. Just write down everything you think you know about yourself. Again, these are all adjectives. Next, you then fill out this sentence: 'since I am this way, I do ?_____' Fill this in with actions.

For example, since I am shy, I don't like speaking in front of crowds. I don't like meeting new people because I feel that it's a burden knowing their names and having to say Hi to them when I come across them. I don't like reaching out to people I don't know because if I see them in an unfamiliar location, I feel I have to reach out and smile and so on forth.

What is important here is you go from the summary description which can be reduced to one adjective and tying it to a long list of actual behaviors. Give yourself time to write this out. What I want you to do is to go from simply summarizing certain aspects of your personality in one word to actually fleshing out that personality trait that you perceive in the form of specific situations.

Once you are done with the step above, the next step is for you to fill out the following statements. These statements are diagnostic in nature. They help you identify triggers that provoke certain actions because you believe those actions emanate from specific parts of your personality. The statement goes like this: 'Since I am this way, I act like this when under these conditions. ' I need you to zero in on the action that you take and then list down the conditions that trigger that action'. Again, since you said that I am this way, I do 1, 2, 3, 4, 5, etcetera, etcetera. Those are actions that you take.

The next step is to identify the triggers for each of those actions. Keep in mind that one action may have many different triggers. This is all self-assessment. You are just basically trying to piece together different aspects of your behavior as well as your emotional and mental triggers so you can understand yourself better. You have to remember that when you feel shy in certain contexts, it is not a foregone conclusion that you have to feel timid. Maybe it is just how you perceive the situation. Perhaps it is because you view certain signals as triggers. What if you were to change your view of those signals? What if they are no longer threatening? What if you started viewing them as positive? Do you see how this works?

The Final Step is to Tie Your Self-conception and Your Triggers and Behaviors with Your Plans for the Future.

Fill out this sentence: 'Since I am this way, these are my plans for the future. 'Be honest with yourself and fill these out. Nobody is going to read these answers except you. You have to be completely honest so you can have an objective and holistic reading of different aspects of your personality. This is crucial for you to re-engineer your self-esteem so you can start acting with more self-confidence.

Is Your Personal Narrative Helping You or Hurting You?

As I have mentioned previously, our personal narrative is a story that we use to make sense of our world. Everything perceived with our five senses are filtered through our minds to create certain judgments. These judgments do not come out of nowhere. They are not automatic because they are strictly a product of us making certain judgment calls based on our personal narrative. We fit the things that we perceive through the story that we carry around and this then guides us on how to interpret these stories and which stories to hang onto and which ones to let go. All-new experiences are filtered through our narrative. In fact, we perceive these stimuli strictly through the judgments made possible by our narrative.

Now, you have to ask yourself since your personal narrative is this powerful, is it helping you or hurting you? The best way to do this is to be mindful of how your narrative is hurting you. Whip out a piece of paper and write down five recent experiences where you felt judged, hurt, humiliated, embarrassed or frustrated by somebody's actions. Write down what happened in terms of who, what, when, where and how. We are looking at factual details here. Do not judge the items. Do not say this person cut me off because he was a jerk. This person cut me off because he thought I was a pushover. No, just describe the scene of a guy in a car cutting you off. That is good enough.

Next, look at how you interpret this situation. What is your default judgment of that situation? How do you normally read these sets of facts? Next, ask yourself is there an alternative explanation? If you are completely honest with yourself, the answer obviously is yes. So, write all of these down. Now, that you have a clear list of all these alternative readings, the next step is to sift through or sort them in terms of empowerment. Which alternative reading would make you feel more empowered?

For example, use the case of the person cutting you off. You could easily read that situation as the person simply having it in for you. That person just intentionally wanted to screw you up. That person intentionally judged as this weak pushover whose day he simply wanted to ruin. Now, look through the alternative readings and ask yourself: Is there a different conclusion?

Well, one obvious alternative is that the person is simply in a hurry. Maybe he got a phone call that his wife just died or somebody in the family got in an accident. If that is the case, you probably would respond very differently. If you knew that for sure, you very likely would feel differently about situation. Instead of feeling insulted or frustrated by the fact that this person cut you off, you probably might even feel happy that he cut you off because he needed to get to where he wanted to go. You would empathize with him because if you were in his same shoes, you would want people to give way. You would want people to fall back because you need to get from point A to point B quickly because somebody died in your family or there was some sort of emergency. Do you see how this works?

Look for an alternative narrative, and here is the secret. There is always an alternative reading. Look for as many different alternative readings and pick the ones that are most empowering. Which are the ones that would make you feel more confident? Which are the ones that would give you a greater sense of self-worth?

Is Your Narrative Truly Yours?

The next step in working with your personal narrative and making very important internal changes is to trace the origin of your narrative. Here is the spoiler. There is no such thing as an original narrative. We always absorb and adopt narratives from somewhere else.

The number one source of our narrative, of course, is our parents. They have a tremendous role in our formative years. We look up to them. They are the source of our initial set of answers. They are the ones in the best position to give us answers that would guide us early on. Since they are our starting point, a lot of us never move past that starting point. We feel that since this is what we were 'born' with, why make the change?

Others seriously question the narratives their parents handed to them to come up with a narrative that better fits their reality. You need to be able to reach that point. You need to be able to understand that just because you have been hanging onto certain narratives for so long, that stubbornness would not necessarily make those narratives productive for you. If you have been wearing chains all this time that prevent you from getting out of the house, it does not really matter that you have worn those chains for 30 years. What matters is that it is preventing you from doing what you want to do. Losing those chains will not be a big deal. In fact, it would be a positive thing.

Use that same mindset when it comes to your narratives. Just because it has been with you for so long, it does not necessarily define you. It is not who you are. It is something that you have picked up along the way. Your identity is what you choose your identity to be. In other words, it is closely tied into your power to choose and your power over your destiny.

What is the bottom line? Claim your own narrative, not the ones you 'inherited'. If you think about it, a lot of these inherited mindsets are simply products of mental and emotional inertia. In other words, we are just mentally and emotionally lazy. We did not get around to questioning these things that we have always assumed to be true about ourselves. This really is too bad because if we were a bit more proactive, we would not suffer from the negative effects of these harmful narratives on our self-esteem. By extension, we would then have greater levels of self-confidence.

The Problem

This is all well and good. The problem is you may not be fully aware of who you are. You might have hidden potential and unless you go through the steps outlined above, it is anybody's guess whether you can wake up to hidden potential. You have to choose to be fully aware of who you are in the here and now.

Pay attention to what you do. Do not just notice the things that you would like to believe about yourself. Do not just dwell on the comforting stories you tell yourself about who you are. This can get a little messy because there are many suppressed memories. There are many coping mechanisms that we hang onto because we feel it would hurt too much to let go of them.

However, if you are suffering from the negative effects of low self-confidence, you really have no choice. You have to wake up to the reality that as painful as it is to let go of what you have, what you stand to gain in terms of personal power and your ability to change your own personal reality is worth far more than what you stand to lose.

Chapter 7: What Can You Be Passionate About?

If you want to build your self-confidence from the inside out, we have to build your self-esteem first. Self-confidence, after all, is just the outside working or the projected version of self-esteem and self-worth. Now, to build up self-esteem, we first need to find what you're passionate about. Find the top 3 things that really excite you. Find the top 3 interests that you would pursue even if you weren't getting paid. Look at what you do. Again, I'm not talking about what you think you should be doing, or what you think you should be going after.

Focus on what you actually do. Look at what you do, and check what kind of interests do you naturally do that you are excited about. Again, these are the things that you invest time and attention in, even if you're not getting paid for it, even if other people aren't giving you respect for it, or give you some sort of appreciation and recognition; it doesn't matter. You just simply are naturally passionate about these things. Find the top 3 things that you are most passionate about.

Now, the next step is to find your hidden potential in your passions. Pull apart what you're interested in. Does it involve planning, execution, problem solving, customization, and improvisation? Look at your interests and see which kinds of personal traits are required for you to pursue that interest.

For example, if you are into running, you probably already know that when people first take up running, it's not easy. They cramp up; they get tired too quickly. In many cases, they get so frustrated that they want to quit. However, there's something about running that keeps you going. There's something about that activity that keeps you engaged enough so you keep doing it over and over until you're able to cover longer and longer distances. Eventually, whatever setbacks you encounter are distant memories because you're constantly able to bounce back from whatever challenges you encounter.

This applies to all interests, whether you're looking at artistic interests, intellectual interests, or interests involving other people. Whatever the case may be, I need you to look at those interests and break them up in terms of these inner strengths of planning, execution, problem solving, customization, improvisation and resilience.

Examine your passions and find what you can love about yourself. When you look at your hidden potentials in your passion, these speak volumes about what you are capable of. You might have a very low view of yourself, but if you were, for example, interested in model building, you would know full well that this kind of interest actually requires a lot of patience. It definitely requires a lot of attention to detail and, in many cases, you have to bounce back from mistakes that you make. The more you do it, the better you get at it.

These interests can tell you a lot about your hidden potentials and hidden traits. You might not think that your resilience or perseverance is a big deal but, believe me, a lot of people don't have those traits. A lot of people don't care to develop those traits, and that's why they struggle. If you have certain hobbies and interests that allow you to scale up your level of resilience, that's something to celebrate. That's definitely something you would want to zero in on and recognize in yourself.

A lot of people don't have the ability to bounce back. A lot of people struggle with having to put in effort day in and day out while the outcome of their project is uncertain. You need to examine your passions and find out what you can love about yourself.

For example, if you love singing, this means that you love the ability to express yourself. You love to take the opportunity to bare your soul to the world. It feels good to let it out; it feels good to express your inner self. Allow yourself to feel good about the fact that you feel good when you do these things.

The bottom line is simple; your passions feel good, and that's perfectly okay. There's no shame in that. You don't have to explain yourself; you don't have to make up excuses why it feels good to engage in your passions. These passions come from somewhere. They are driven by an inner drive. There's no need to deny these inner drives; there's no need to be ashamed of them.

For example, if you like to sing in the shower, maybe it's because you like to fantasize being in front of a massive audience and making them feel good through a well-sung song makes you feel good, and that's perfectly okay. There's no right or wrong answer here; there's nothing to be ashamed of.

Look at the top 3 things that you're passionate about, and I just need you to break them down as to the traits that they involve. Once these traits are crystal clear to you, dig even deeper. What do these traits mean? What does your passion involving these traits say about your character and your values?

Personal Realization List

By this point, certain things should be clear in your mind. You should be able to connect the dots in terms of what you're passionate about, your interests, your character and values.

In this step, I want you to formalize this connection. Now this doesn't have to be all scientific. This doesn't have to meet the rigorous standards of clinical psychology; that's besides the point. The point here is for you to realize that your passions reveal part of your character.

I need you to complete these three sentences. I need you to write down the phrase:

"I love (put your passion here) because it shows (part of your character)".

I need you to repeat that sentence three times and fill it in. Of course, tie it into the top 3 interests that I asked you to examine earlier. The bottom line should be simple, when you look at these three statements, what they're really saying is that: "I celebrate myself when I practice my passion".

When you practice your passion, you are in your own little world. You're doing your own thing and its perfectly okay. You're celebrating who you are, and you're tapping into a lot of personal traits that are very important to develop. These traits can actually help you in many areas of your life. In fact, they may reveal certain hidden potential you may not have allowed yourself to become aware of.

Find the Top 3 Things You Fear About Yourself

At the other end of the equation, I also need you to look at the things that you normally avoid. For example, you don't like public speaking. What is it about public speaking that really turns you off? There are many intelligent people with great voices and great personas who can definitely project the persona to the crowd, but are still very uncomfortable with speaking in public.

It's not because they don't have the raw ingredients to speak well in public. It's not because they are unable to do it if the circumstances are right. They just don't want to. Now, I just want you to zero in on why you don't want to do certain things. Start from the things you constantly wish to avoid and then try to pick them apart. What is it about them that really turns you off?

Now, when you break down these activities, they should also, like the exercise above, reveal certain traits. These are traits that are triggered by the activity. Now, you should then ask yourself: "What kind of hidden potential is there that I already have, but I can only express if I overcome my fear?"

For example, going back to the public speaking scenario, if you are blessed with a great voice and amazing stage presence, but at the same time, you're scared stiff of speaking in front of a public audience, it really is a shame. Why? You have the equipment. You have the voice; you have the presence. However, there is one setback; you are not mentally allowing yourself to find the courage to speak up in front of a crowd. The hidden potential here, of course, should be obvious. You have the voice. You have the presence. You can make this work except for that one problematic part.

You need to zero in on these and have a clear idea of what your full list of potential traits are. Maybe you have the potential for building great things. Maybe you have the potential for being nurturing and patient with people. Maybe you have the potential for cultivating others, so they can become great leaders. Whatever the case may be, I need you to zero in on your hidden potential. These are the list of potentials that you are not aware of, or you don't allow yourself to become aware of. You need to do this using the proactive technique above and the reactive technique, which is to analyze the activities that you routinely fear.

Chapter 8: Fine-tune Your Passions to Build Self-Esteem

Now that you have a clear idea of what your hidden potentials are, I need you to step back and allow yourself to feel good about them. This shows you in no uncertain terms that you're not worthless, not by a long shot. You have the potential to be somebody great. You have the raw ingredients. It's there; it's just beneath the surface. In many cases, you just don't want to become aware of it, but it's there.

I need you to recognize the list of your hidden and obvious potential. Now, look at that list and allow yourself to feel good. Allow yourself to come to the conclusion that you're not completely worthless, that there's nothing wrong with you and that there's nothing missing with you. You have the raw ingredients for success.

Of course, to turn potential into reality takes work. It takes attention to detail, and it takes perseverance and consistency. Still, it's a tremendous victory for you to even recognize that you have all these things going for you. There's no need for false modesty. There's no need to sabotage a positive feeling by saying: "Well, everybody has potential". or "I'm just a face in the crowd because everybody has potential that they're not developing."

Forget that. Just focus on the fact that you have this potential and you have the choice to develop them so you can live up to your fullest capability. You have it in you. This proves point blank that you have the ingredients for greatness, you just need to connect the dots; you just need to mix the ingredients.

In other words, you just need to act on what you already have. It's not like you're going to have to proactively get something that you currently don't possess. It's already there. I need you to wrap your mind around this, and I need you to feel good about it. It's something to be celebrated; it's something to feel happy about. This is part of who you are and what you have to offer the universe. The next step is to look at these raw ingredients and build on them.

Take Your Passions and Build on Them

Develop yourself by developing your passions. If you're passionate about certain activities, then pursue them by all means. The more you do something that gives you fulfillment and happiness, the more you invest in your personal purpose. The more you do it, the more you invest in your self-esteem.

How does this work? Well, it's very simple; the more you develop your passions, the more competent you are with them. They're no longer just potential; this is no longer just a theoretical set of traits that would be nice to develop. When you work on them, and you sharpen them and build them, they affect your reality because you can see their impact.

For example, if you like to sing in the shower, you might want to pursue your passion for singing. You can start out of the shower, take some singing lessons and then venture out to open mike night at a local club, bar or hall. Now, everybody's lined up to sing so you don't need to feel out of place.

However, when you get up there, and you face that crowd and you just bare your soul that is a tremendous victory. Because you're not doing it for them; you're doing it for yourself. You are doing it to follow the process. You've come from somebody who is hiding this immense personal light under a bowl by singing in the shower, to somebody who actually found the nerve to sing in front of the public. That's a victory. It doesn't really matter what happens next, what matters is that you were able to make that journey. That is a massive transition.

You celebrate yourself when you develop your passions. This is extremely important because the more you celebrate yourself, the more it sinks in. However, there's nothing wrong with you. You are worth respecting, you are worth loving, and you are worth something. The more you accept yourself, the more your self-esteem grows. The secret here is to be mindful of the process. This is crucial; you're not just enjoying the journey.

Now, don't get me wrong, there's a lot of value in that. But this is purposeful; you must also pay attention to the character you're building. You know you're doing this for a reason; you're doing this because you have low self-esteem, and you want to build it up and transform it so it can project into greater and greater levels of self-confidence. This is very hard to do unless you keep a laser focus on your transition from somebody who's shy and suffering from feelings of inadequacy and low self-worth, to somebody who feels that they can actively change their waking reality. In other words, somebody who is operating from a place of tremendous self-confidence.

Self-Esteem is Based on Accomplishment

Now, a lot of people might think that this is bad news. After all, we live in a modern society where self-confidence is supposed to be a door prize. If you've gone to a public school in the United States, you know exactly what I'm talking about. Most school curriculum emphasizes self-confidence instead of making sure kids go through the traditional curriculum to achieve academic excellence. The old standard actually had it right. Self-confidence comes later; there is a precursor to self-confidence.

It's like building a massive tower. You can't build the tower on sand; it's going to sink. It's going to tip over and kill people inside the tower. I mean, this is common sense. By the same token, you can't just build self-confidence without a foundation. What are you going to build your self-confidence on? And that's why you need to first focus on your passions, your interests, discover more about it and then make the transition from feeling good about your potential, challenging your potential, celebrating your potential and celebrating yourself to self-confidence.

In other words, you need to do something with your passions first. This is where objectivity comes in. Like I said earlier, the world doesn't care about your feelings, all it cares about is what you actually do or what you actually achieve. By entertaining your passions, polishing them, and engaging in them, you start accomplishing things. You start getting good at your interests.

Again, taking the example of singing, it's one thing to sing in the shower and have the voice of a small puppy being tortured to death. It's great you're getting in touch with your inner passions. It's great that you've identified your need to bare your soul through singing. However, you can't leave it there. You have to actually polish your passion. You have to get good at it. If your voice sounds like a small puppy being tortured to death, then you need to keep working on your passion until you sound good.

You see how this works? This is where accomplishment comes in; this is where the real world steps in. It's easy to feel good about subjective things like, oh, you just have to get in touch with your passion, and you just have to bare your soul by entertaining your passion. That's all well and good behind closed doors, but ultimately, you have to have an external validation.

In other words, you have to get good enough at it so you can objectively say I've accomplished something. I've taken something that I was interested in and passionate about and I have worked on it to such a degree that other people would agree that I am good at it. In other words, I have achieved. This is crucial because otherwise, all this progress would simply be subjective. It would just simply be self-serving and private. That's not going to move the needle as far as your self-esteem goes.

Real self-esteem is built on accomplishment. When you become good at something, you allow yourself to feel good at it and say to yourself: "I'm actually good at something. I'm actually accomplished at something." By doing so, you carve out your own personal space; this is one space that nobody can take away from you because you worked at it. You see how this works?

Self-esteem is based on accomplishment. It is not some a priori value that somebody just drops on you because you showed up. It's not a door prize; it's built on something solid. In other words, you worked at it and that's what makes it real. You have to keep working on your passions; you have to get good at them. I know this is going to be a little bit touchy. I know this is going to be painful for many people reading this, but I need to say it. You have to allow yourself, after a certain point, to be critiqued. You have to subject yourself to an objective standard. Prior to this point, everything is subjective everything is all about your feelings. How it feels great, how you feel validated, how you feel honored; that's all well and good.

However, the moment you take your passion and subject it to external review, that's when you know when you have truly accomplished it or not. If not, that's okay. This is where the trait of resilience comes in. You hit a bump on the road and suffer a setback; that's okay. You need to go back, keep working, try again until you succeed. Be open to adjustment and fine-tuning. Don't fear judgment; don't fear critique. Get good; aim to be the best in what you're passionate about. Use your passion as fuel to do whatever it takes or however long it takes until you get good.

Let's face it, when you're working on something, there are many days where you don't want to try. There are many days where you just want to give up. This is where honest passion comes in. Because if you're truly passionate, you would draw from that internal energy and get the power you need to keep pushing.

Build on the Objective Foundation of Excellence

When you become excellent at something, you feel more confident. You have solid and objective foundation for this self-assessment that you are good at something. It's not just wishful thinking; you're not just hypnotizing yourself or engaging in self-delusion. This is real because it can be traced to real accomplishments. Compare this with showing up at a school and everybody getting an A, or participating in a sport and nobody loses because everybody gets a medal. The sense of accomplishment in that context is destroyed. There's nothing to work for because whether you try hard and sacrifice, or slack off, the end result is the same.

That's not the way the real world works. The real world gives you the right to feel good about yourself because you have something objectively to feel good about. In other words, it's based on a solid foundation of accomplishment.

You're Only As Good As Your Last Victory

Now, if you think that the previous section is a little bit trying, I've got some bad news for you, it gets a little bit worse. The truth is, you're only as good as your last victory.

When was the last time you hung out with people that keep reminiscing about the good old days? They would tell you: "Oh yeah, five years ago I was making a million bucks a month," or "Ten years ago, I was traveling all over the world".

While those kinds of statements may be great in terms of rehashing shared memories, sooner or later, they get old and stale. In fact, they can get downright annoying. You see, the world not only focuses on the results that you produce, it also focuses on the here and now. In other words, can you produce good results now? While the gravity and enormous value of what you did in the past does hold some sway, the more distant the accomplishment, the less the world cares. It has a short-term memory, like it or not.

This is why you need to understand that when it comes to producing accomplishment, you're only as good as your last victory. Don't rest on your laurels. Allow yourself to be constantly engaged, constantly refine your skill sets, challenge yourself continuously. This leads to continuous improvement; you're always looking for the next bigger and better thing to do as far as your passions go. This gives you a tremendous competitive advantage compared to people who are trying to do what you're doing. They can't hold the candle to you if you are really passionate about this because you are constantly improving yourself. The difference is like black and white because you are invested in constant improvement.

Ride the Spiral Staircase to Greater Self-Esteem

Believe it or not, constant improvement on your passion leads to greater and greater self-esteem. It starts with your passions. You then improve on them so you produce better and better results. You then get some objective validation. People would tell you: "Wow! You're singing better now than before," or "You're making more money now than before," or "You're living in a bigger house now than before," or "You're more respected now than before".

Whatever the case may be, and whatever your passion may be, there's an increase in objective validation. This then boosts your self-esteem because you tell yourself in no uncertain terms, "I'm doing something right. I took my passions, improved on it, and I can objectively test that I've reached a higher level.

When you feel greater self-esteem, your level of passion increases; your passion "gas tank" is refilled, and you have more energy to go to the next level of improved action, objective validation, and on and on it goes. It's an upward spiral of greater and greater self-esteem. With each increase, there's also a greater projection, meaning there's an outward manifestation; your self-confidence is more apparent.

People who are good at what they're doing become more and more confident. It gets harder and harder for them to hide and explain away. The more confident they become, the more successful they become because the world sits up and pays attention. See how the upward spiral works?

Chapter 9: What's Holding You Back?

Now that you have a clear understanding of how to build on your passions to boost your self-esteem so you can become more confident, the next step is to identify things that are preventing you from taking action in the here and now. You have to ask yourself: "What's holding me back? If I know all these things to be true, why am I not taking action now?" Well, if you were to write down all your limitations, it's very easy to come up with a list. Most people can easily come up with a list.

For example, they would say: "I had a bad childhood. My parents left me", "I was born with the disability; I have a learning disability", "People were mean to me in the past", "I can't get a break", "I'm just unlucky", on and on it goes.

Now, what you need to do is just write down all the reasons why you think you can't take action now. Just get it off your chest. This probably will take several days; it's not going to happen overnight, so give yourself some time. Just think: "Why am I not taking action now? If I know all these things to be true, that it would lead to greater self-confidence, what's holding me back?"

Write all of these down and give yourself several days. After that period of time, you should have a fairly long list. In fact, if you read through this, it might even seem impossible. It might seem so restricted that you are just basically bucking against the tide that you have no chance against.

Now, here's an eye-opener; I need you to look at the list and then filter them into two categories: real limitations and imagined limitations. Real limitations are actual physical, legal, or political limitations. In other words, there's a law saying you shouldn't take action, or there's a person pointing a gun at you, saying: "If you do this, I will kill you." Or you have a disability which makes it impossible to do. That is a "real" limitation. Everything else, you need to push aside to be imagined limitations.

Now that you have sorted it, look at your list. You would notice that there are a few items under "real limitations." If you're completely honest with yourself, there are only a few items there. Everything else is under imagined limitations. Now, even with your real limitations, there are always alternatives. There are always workarounds; there are always substitutes. My point here is not to make you feel bad and make you feel like you're giving yourself excuses. My point here is not to emotionally beat you up. My point here is to let you know that your limitations are only as big as you think they are; that's the only way they would really have any hold on you. I hope you understand this.

The truth is, there are few real limitations. The old saying: "If there's a will, there's a way" is absolutely true. You might think that these limitations are very formidable. You might think that these limitations make it all but impossible to do certain things but believe me, if you really wanted to do them, you will find a way. Maybe you can say you don't have any money. Maybe you can say that you don't have any time. But guess what, there are always substitutes. You can work with other people. You could come up with creative solutions. If there is a will, there is a way. The real limitation here is that you don't feel that you have the willpower needed to overcome these limitations.

So at the end of this discussion, I want you to absorb what I have just said and then look at your list again. If you are completely honest with yourself, there would be very, very few items left under "real limitations." In fact, I would argue that for most people, there would be absolutely zero real limitations. Once you get to zero, you know you have reached a turning point. So kick this idea around your mind, go through this process over and over again until you truly believe that there are no limitations holding you back.

What's Making You Wait?

The next step of the analysis is to confront our normal tendency to wait. Make no mistake about it, whenever you're working on something important in your life, the normal human tendency is to wait. In other words, we're trying to kick the can down the road; we're trying to give ourselves excuses for not taking action, and trying to hold things off. This is perfectly natural; this is to be expected. Why?

As I have mentioned previously, people are creatures of habit. Change terrifies us. We get set in our ways. Once we do things a certain way, it really takes quite a bit of effort if you want to change. So it's really important to understand that this is going on. The more you wait, the more you are basically giving in to your mind's efforts at holding you back because it's scared. It doesn't know what's around the corner; it's uncertain. It needs to be in control, but it can't be in control because it doesn't have all the information. So you are playing mind games with yourself; it all manifests itself in waiting.

There's another variation to this, a lot of people would like to trick themselves into thinking that they're actually taking action by collecting information. What they're doing is a classic response called Analysis Paralysis. The thesis behind this thinking is that as long as you are researching pooling information from everywhere, you are working towards your goals.

I'm sorry, but you're just fooling yourself if you think this way. What you're doing is you are giving yourself an excuse not to take action. There's a fatal flaw to the thesis. The thesis basically states that if you have all the information, things will become certain. In other words, once you take action on your plan, because you have all the facts under your control, it will be a slam dunk. Well, life doesn't work that way; there is always uncertainty. Certain things might still pop up; certain things that you didn't expect might materialize and these can get in the way of your success. That's just the way life is. Life isn't perfect. We live in an imperfect world.

So the whole idea of waiting because you are just gathering information is a nonstarter. It doesn't help you. You're just going around in circles; you are just fooling yourself. So you have to honestly ask yourself what you are you waiting for. What's making you wait? What exactly are you doing that you're not taking action now? You have a clear idea from the information I gave you in previous chapters. Now that you have that information in your hands, why are you not implementing it? What's making you wait?

Time for Some Real Talk

Unfortunately, if people have a tough time getting from point A to point B, sometimes they need a push; sometimes they require a much-needed jolt to wake them up. So here's some real talk. Your hurdles are only as big as you choose to see them. You may be imagining all these things that are holding you back. You may be imagining that all these contingencies are pushing you to wait and put off your plan of building on your self-esteem and self-confidence. What you're really doing is you're giving yourself reasons not to try.

The real talk here is quite simple, you got so used to the personal reality that you live in, that as unpleasant as it may be, it's your reality. It's something that you're accustomed to; it's something that you feel holds few surprises for you. After all, you lived this life for a long time. You're not happy, you know you're living way below your fullest potential, but this is something that's familiar. I need you to realize this. I need you to confront this and stare it straight on, call it by its proper name. Label this correctly because if this is what you're dealing with, you're really just dealing with fear, which is manifested in a lot of ways, and one of them is laziness. You're lazy regarding personal change.

Instead of training your personal resources to come up with ways to make the transition, you deflect the issue. You spend your energies of thinking up a billion reasons for not trying. You focus on the obstacles ahead. You focus on how hard it can be to change yourself. You also start thinking of a billion reasons not to start now, even if you are completely on board regarding the wisdom of this program. Your mind can still play tricks on you by focusing on reasons why you should kick the can down the road. You would say to yourself: "I completely agree, but not now," and then you would rattle off all sorts of reasons why you should not start now.

Just Do It

So what's the solution to constantly holding this inner debate in your head regarding when to start and why you should start? The resolution is simple; it's actually the same solution used by Alexander the Great. In one of his travels, Alexander the Great was given access to the Gordian Knot. According to legend, whoever solves the Gordian Knot will conquer.

So what did Alexander the Great do? He didn't sit down and try to unbraid the knot, spend a tremendous amount of time and sweat buckets to fix it. Instead, he took out his sword and just cut it in half. In the same way, you can agonize over the intricacies of your personal issues. You can give yourself reason after reason for not starting. You can dwell on your inner limitations. You can analyze all the external circumstances that you will be facing. Well, I'm telling you, if you do that, you're just making them bigger. Their hold on you becomes stronger and stronger. You end up magnifying them. The solution is actually quite simple, just do it.
Just like Alexander the Great, take action. Don't focus on the details. Don't agonize over the consequences; just resolve to start

now. That's how you build self-esteem. You have to understand that self-esteem is built on competence. When you feel that you could do certain things right, day in and day out, you become confident about your ability to bring about certain results. That's how self-esteem is built; it's built on the solid foundation of accomplishment. All the pep talk in the world is not going to do you much good. All the positive self-affirmations of you talking to the mirror is not going to help if you just keep it all inside. You have to act on it.

When you start pursuing your passions now so you become objectively good at them, you build competence. Competence, in turn, leads to greater and greater levels of confidence. You're able to change your world in a positive way. This is not self-hypnosis. This is not you playing mental tricks on yourself. You can actually see the results in objective reality.

People tell you- you're a good singer. People tell you-you take great pictures. People tell you- you know how to make money. Whatever passion you have, there is an objective benchmark, and you can see that this benchmark is real. You can point to it; you can experience it. This then leads to greater and greater self-confidence because you are aware that you have an impact on your external world.

People do pay attention to what you do. People do appreciate what you do. However, you can't stop. You can't just hit a home run and call it a day. You have to keep swinging. It requires continuous action. If you were to do this, then your tendency to balk becomes weaker and weaker. In fact, at a certain point, it would actually take more willpower to stop than to start.

The Secret: Start With Your Passions

To recap, if you want to build self-esteem so you can have greater self-confidence, start with your passions. The reason why you should start with your passions is that its internal, it's all about you; it's personal. There are no right or wrong answers. You do the choosing; you're the one in the driver's seat. It's also non-threatening because it starts internally.

You can pick your internal passions. Nobody can dictate to you what your passions are. Nobody can dictate to you what you should be good at. The fact that you start from an inner space of control makes this whole initial stage non-threatening. There's no competition at this point because your choice is your choice. It makes sense for you, and it's completely unique to you. You own it. You don't owe anybody anything. It's completely yours.

Next, you celebrate yourself when you work on your passions. It's something particular to you. It's something that you draw a lot of enjoyment for; you own it 100%. After this, you scale it up, the more time, effort and attention to detail you devote your passions, the better you get at it, and then you scale it up to the point that it becomes more and more public. The more public it becomes, the more external validation you get.

Now, I'm not going to lie to you and tell you that this is a simple matter of going from point A to point B. This doesn't happen overnight. This is not an instant home run situation. It's not like you step up to the plate, swing the bat and the ball shoots out of the park; it doesn't work that way. In many cases, you have to take many, many swings until you get a pop fly. It still gets caught and you strike out, but it's a start.

This is where passion comes in. You really do things that you're passionate about because there would be setbacks along the way. There will be bumps along the road; you just have to keep at it one step at the time. Eventually, you get better and better with each step and then you start scaling up. The whole process becomes more and more public, and the more public validation you get, the greater your self-confidence becomes.

Chapter 10: Project Your Celebration of Your Impact on Others

The reason why building on self-esteem has a public dimension is because the things that you do, as far as your passions go, ultimately have an impact on the lives of others. When you get good at something, it will ultimately affect other people. This is a good thing. You should not keep it private because when it's private, there is really no external validation. It's just your own personal, little, private thing, and it's really not going to do you much good in terms of your self-confidence. Why? You're taking out the external validation part of the upward spiral.

You're just saying to yourself: "This is good. I'm happy with this". Well, the moment you step out into the public square, and people compare you to other people with similar passions, chances are quite good that you might not measure up. All these good feelings that you built come crashing down like a house of cards. So you have to let in external validations and metric systems. You have to compare yourself to others with the same passion. In other words, your accomplishments must be based on objective standards. If you're really good, others will be positively impacted. Your positive impact on others is a crucial component of building self-esteem.

The external validation process is just a feedback mechanism. It just tells you that if your passion, seemingly subjective as it is, can actually be objectively judged to be good. That's when you know you actually have a real accomplishment. Otherwise, you're just playing games with yourself; otherwise, this is just all subjective.

Again, I can't repeat this enough, your positive impact on others is a crucial component for building self-esteem. You get a feedback mechanism when you see that other people are positively impacted by this. If you love to sing, they love hearing you sing. Their day is much better because they heard your voice. If you like to provide a service like making pizza, their day is better because they have a yummy pizza. They love pizza, and you give them a pizza that tastes so good to them. You see how this works?

Building self-esteem can't be a self-absorbed and a totally self-enclosed process. It's not a closed loop. There is always an external validation aspect to it. This is nothing to be afraid of; this is nothing to run away from. In fact, you should accept it and embrace it because it leads to a feedback mechanism that pushes you to try harder and harder, to give your very best. Put simply, real self-esteem has an objective impact. It isn't just about self-programming. It isn't just about you entertaining your subjective reality. It is real precisely because others are impacted positively. The key word here is positively, that's how you know you've accomplished something.

For example, your passion is making home-brewed beer. Well, you can brew beer for yourself and let's face it, objectively it might taste really nasty in the beginning. But unless you allow yourself to be critiqued by other people who like beer, you're not going to make any progress. So in the beginning, people might reject your beer and say: "Man, it tastes horrible".

However, by pursuing your passion, you try again and again until the beer tastes great. The moment people say to you: "This is amazing beer," your self-esteem blows up. It skyrockets because now, you could objectively base your increased self-esteem on a standard that everybody would agree on. Your passion for making home-brewed beer has a positive impact on the lives of people. They like your stuff, so you can feel better and better about yourself. You then realize you're not completely worthless. You then realize you're actually good at something instead of feeling inadequate all the time. You see how this works?

This internal build-up of self-esteem leads to greater and greater levels of self-confidence. Because the moment you know you're good at creating beer, you can then create other types of beer, or you could step up the quality of the beer that you're crafting. The better and better your product gets, the more confident you become until you eventually reach a point where you feel that the moment you make a batch of beer that it's going to be good. You can say this confidently because you have paid your dues. You know what to do, and you know what not to do when it comes to making beer.

Allow Yourself To Feel Great When You're Impacting Others Positively

I can't emphasize this point enough. There are a people are smart. There are a lot of people who are beautiful. There are a lot of people who are athletic. However, the problem is they still have low self-esteem because they don't allow themselves to realize that their intelligence, their beauty, their skills and their passions have a positive impact on others. They let their inner subjective reality get the better of them.

You'd be surprised how some people feel that regardless of how many medals, awards they get, and money they make, they're still worthless. They're still a big fat zero. There are many people like this. Don't be one of those people. Allow yourself to feel great that you are impacting others positively.

Now, in the big scheme of things, your beer might not be at the same level as Sam Adams, and that's perfectly okay. As long as you know that your passions are impacting others positively, that's perfectly fine. Accept the positive feelings, you're entitled to it. Don't feel that just because your parents told you that you're worthless, ugly, stupid, that is your reality. Just because you had a nasty boss in the past that diminished you and crushed your ego doesn't mean that's the only level you can function at.

Accept the positive feelings people give you. If they tell you: "This pasta is great", say: "Thank you", and let the feeling sink in. If somebody tells you have a great singing voice, accept the complement. Don't deflect the complement. I see this all the time. For example, somebody would complement you on your great lasagna, and then you would say, "Well, thanks, but I didn't put in all the right ingredients", or "The ingredients weren't that fresh". What's wrong with this picture? Why not just accept the complement that person was positively impacted by what you did and that's perfectly fine. Leave it at that level.

It doesn't have to be perfect. You don't have to compare yourself to master chefs. You see how this works? Whatever you do, accept the positive feeling. There's no space for shame, guilt or regret in this situation. Those emotions might be default emotions, but you cannot let them rob you of your personal victory. Also, stop comparing yourself to others. They may have a greater impact on others, so what.

What's important is that you made a positive impact on others as well. Just because other people cook better lasagna than you, doesn't take away from the fact that your lasagna is good. Accept the fact that it's good. Accept that other people lack the taste and leave it at that. Stop comparing yourself to "perfect people." That's a sure way of snatching defeat from the jaws of victory. Don't do that. What's important is that you are clear about a core competency that you have. You have to allow yourself to feel valuable so you can start to act like a valuable person.

The Genesis of Self-Confidence

Project your self-worth outward. Now that you know that you have a positive impact on people, allow yourself to feel good about it. Understand that not everyone can do what you do. You have value. You have a right to feel good about yourself. You have a right for a place in this world. You have a right to claim your place. You are entitled to stake your place. Understand all of these; accept all of these. There's no shame in feeling good about your capabilities and capacities. Remember this.

If you come from a religious tradition that looks down on bragging, or maybe you come from a cultural background that is big on modesty. Well, set that aside for a second. Understand that when you fall prey to false modesty, your self-confidence is the first casualty.

In another way, you're not exercising modesty when you constantly feel bad about your capabilities. When you feel like a complete and total loser, you're not practicing modesty. So it's okay to feel that you are good at something. It's okay to feel that you're even the best at something. Defeat false modesty because it's not helping you right now. Defeat faulty programming that depresses self-esteem and self-confidence. Maybe your parents said: "don't brag." Maybe your parents said: "don't boast." Well, when it comes to building a healthy self-esteem and self-confidence, maybe it's time to brag a little. Maybe it's time to crow about your accomplishments. You have to remember that you're trying to build better self-confidence so you could impact the world better.

In other words, the philosophy behind modesty is the same, which is to get along better with other people, to impact other people better. The objective is the same, but the problem is you're not achieving that objective when you constantly beat up yourself. That's why you need to constantly defeat false modesty and faulty programming that depresses self-esteem and self-confidence. This will then enable you to speak up about your accomplishments. You can then say to people: "yeah, I make great lasagna", or "I know how to sing", or "I know how to trade stock", whatever your passions are, it's okay to talk about your accomplishments and your passions.

Keep in mind that this is different from bragging. Bragging is when there is no accomplishment. Bragging is when you just say, "I am a better singer than Elvis". When people listen to you on a purely objective level, you sound like a puppy that's being tortured slowly to death. Do you see the disconnect here?

It's one thing to speak up about your accomplishments based on solid objective evidence. Ironically, a lot of people with low self-confidence are big braggers, because that's one way they cope with their low self-confidence. They don't want to go through the time, effort and process of actually building real self-confidence. So they prefer shortcuts, they prefer to brag; they prefer to talk big. However, the problem is they're not basing this exaggerated assessment of their capabilities on anything real. You are, because you are simply speaking up about objective accomplishments.

This issue of bragging deserves its own section. That's why you need to keep reading below.

Bragging Vs Confidence

Let me recap, bragging is based on accomplishments. or grossly exaggerated accomplishments. Confidence, on the other hand, is based on the real impact you have on other people. Confidence is based on the real value people place on your impact on them. You need to know the difference.

Again, people with low self-confidence are actually drawn to bragging because it's a quick, easy and lazy way to feel good about themselves, but what they're really doing is just hypnotizing themselves or deluding themselves into feeling good because there's really nothing to feel good about. There are no accomplishments there. Worse yet, a lot of people who like to brag often feel they have to drag down other people's accomplishments.

She doesn't know how to sing that well. So what does she do? She bashes a truly good singer she knows so she can feel good about her own abilities. I'm telling you, that destructive behavior doesn't really do you and other people any good. Know the difference between bragging and real confidence. You are confident because you have something to be confident about. You're confident because you have value, and you have proven to yourself to have that value through objective accomplishments. You have proven that you can contribute to other people. There's no shame in feeling this type of confidence.

Chapter 11: Project What You Want to See

What you see or perceive you see impacts your confidence. Do not think that you are being weak or being emotional if you see something that you do not like, and it torpedoes your self-confidence. Understand that this is completely human. Understand that there is nothing wrong with you if you feel or react this way. The truth is whatever we see or think we see impacts our confidence. The things that we perceive send us signals that tell us certain things about ourselves. Depending on how you interpret this information, it can be a positive thing, or it can be a negative thing as far as your self-confidence goes.

The truth is you are always editing your reality. If you were to take people and give them the same signals, and they come from two totally different families, chances are quite good they would come up with two entirely distinct interpretations. Now, both those interpretations are logical. Both of them are rational and sound. In other words, the two interpretations are correct, but they are still different from each other. This highlights our ability to edit our reality. Every single time your body is picking signals from the outside world, you only choose to become aware of a tiny fraction of those signals. Of the signals that you do dwell on, you choose to interpret them in a certain way.

Again, two totally different people can focus on the same facts and walk away with two completely diverse interpretations. This is all due to personal judgment. A personal judgment does not come in a vacuum. It is a reflection of who we are inside. In other words, our personal narrative dramatically impacts how we choose to judge our reality. That is why I can say confidently that we are always editing our reality. Just because you live with certain circumstances does not necessarily mean that there is only one way of responding to those circumstances. Always be aware of this because you invariably have the power of choice. You can always choose to edit your reality in such a way that it boosts your self-confidence instead of undermines it.

For example, if you were to show up at Starbucks, and you meet two people, and one of them looks at you with wide-open eyes and a half smile; the other one squints at you with their eyebrows furrowed. When you look at these two people, it is too easy to think that you somehow some way offended them. Maybe you were wearing an inappropriate shirt, or perhaps you said something; possibly you moved in a certain way; however, it is quite simple to interpret this scenario as you having rubbed them the wrong way.

If you were to look at the same facts, you can also conclude that they possibly had a tough day. Perhaps they are friends, who just had a nasty argument, and they are basically heated and a lot of this emotional turbulence can still be detected on their faces. The way they look has nothing to do with what you are doing. The reason why they look the way they look is because of their interaction.

Those are two totally different interpretations of the same group of facts. Let me ask you which interpretation is more empowering? Which interpretation would have a more positive or at least a neutral impact on your self-confidence? The choice should be obvious. It would be choice #2. In other words, it is not about you. Maybe they are just having a tough time. Perhaps they simply had a nasty argument. Whatever the case, it has nothing to do with you.

If you were to take the first interpretation, it is easy to feel beat up. It is tempting to feel small, discouraged, diminished and depressed. Why? You meet these people, and they judge you. Somehow, some way they do not approve of you, and you are to blame. As a result, your self-confidence takes a hit. Since you are always editing your reality, always make it a point to pick the most empowering yet realistic interpretation of situations you experience. In other words, make it a habit of picking certain facts to support an empowering interpretation.

Going back to that Starbucks example, when you walk in, and you notice that they have been talking to each other or they are raising their voices, use that fact to support interpretation #2. Try to look for other pieces of evidence to support a more empowering interpretation. The secret is not to fool yourself. The secret here is not to play games with yourself by making up evidence.

Instead, your empowering interpretation must be realistic. In other words, it must be based on solid evidence so look for things that exist. Look for proof that they are frazzled, that they just had an argument; that they are feeling under the weather. Whatever the case may be, come up with evidence that supports that. When you are able to do that, and you become even more confident because you know that you are not just playing mind games with yourself. You know that this alternative interpretation is based on reality. This then not only preserves your confidence but allows it to grow.

Quick Recap: How Judgment Works

Let me expand on the themes I have raised earlier in this book and earlier in this chapter. I need you to get a crystal clear understanding of how judgment works so you can make it work for you instead of against you. Your body is a neutral data collector. All data is neutral. Seriously. The things that we see, smell, taste, hear and touch are all neutral. I know it is hard to believe but if you really think about it, they are all neutral.

What makes them stressful, distressing or positive and uplifting is your interpretation. Your mind is constantly judging. It judges on two levels. First, it looks at all the information that your body picks up and chooses to dwell on certain things. These things are only a small fraction of all the signals your body picks up throughout the day. It then goes onto the next level of judging the information that it dwells on. You interpret all this data either positively, negatively or neutrally.

Your judgment depends on your personality. It is the filter that you use to edit your world. If your personal narrative is that you are an ugly person; you have a bad personality or people do not like you because you are worthless and unwanted then you probably would look at this otherwise neutral data in a very negative way. If your personal narrative is that you are a person who is worth respecting and a person of accomplishment, and that you can make positive changes in the world and people like you, you very likely would have a more favorable interpretation. Do you see how this works?

All this information is constantly being filtered through your personality. Your judgment then impacts your reality. How? When you make a judgment initially, it remains emotional. It remains in the realm of the intellectual and feelings. However, when you make a judgment of your thoughts, it is easy to become emotional.

For example, you meet somebody, and they give a neutral look. They look at you, and you interpret it as this person thinks I am ugly, and you feel emotionally upset so you take action, and you call her a bitch or you get up, and you feel bad about yourself and your blood pressure is raised; you begin to sweat, and you are angry. These actions impact your world because you go from the purely internal and emotional to the realm of reality where the world sits up and pays attention. In other words, you take action. That is where the world reacts.

Again, I cannot emphasize this enough. The world is subjective. It only cares about the actions that you take and the words you say. So, the moment you say, "You're a bitch!" because you feel that she thinks you are ugly, you have taken action, and there will be consequences because the world is going to react. This probably a negative impact on her, and she might respond adversely. Do you see how this works? You can also choose to respond in a different way.

The Good News

The good news in this whole process is that you can always choose your judgments. Do not think that your judgments are foregone conclusions. The worst trick you can ever play on yourself is you think that there is only one way to judge certain information. You can always choose what you perceive. You can consistently choose what you focus on. You can definitely choose your judgments. It is easy to say this, but it is hard to practice this. I will be the first to admit that; however, you need to get on it. You need to keep practicing.

The moment you start perceiving certain things, and you are beginning to judge, ask yourself is there an alternative reading. When this chick at Starbucks looks at me weird does it necessarily mean that I am a bad person? Does it inevitably mean that there is something wrong with me or that there is something missing in me? Look for alternative reading. The good news is that there is always an alternative reading available. The secret here is to make sure that the alternative reading is based on facts.

So, look for facts that would support your alternative reading. Ultimately the more you do this, the further you change your narrative. The more you do this, the greater you judge based on the narrative you want to set for yourself. This is a point of victory because you are conscious about your narrative. You no longer feel like you are a slave to certain automatic interpretations.

Believe me a lot of those automatic interpretations you may have inherited from your parents. Maybe they are negative programming that you have picked up along the way. Whatever the case may be; you have the power of choice in the here and now. If those narratives are not serving you, you can drop them and replace them with another set of narratives.

Sound Judgments Vs Delusions

I cannot emphasize this enough. If you are going to be looking for alternative readings, search for facts that would support your alternative readings. This way, you do not feel that you are just tricking yourself. You do not feel that you are merely deluding yourself and lying to yourself. You have to look for sound judgments based on the evidence that you find. You then build on your strengths. You are not tricking yourself into thinking that you have certain qualities that you do not actually have. Instead, you are being realistic while at the same time allowing yourself to look at your situation in a positive light.

This is really important because sound judgment, since they are objective, opens you up to correction and improvement. Delusions, on the other hand, are simply feel-good mechanisms. You are just making things up, and you are just choosing to lie to yourself and, ultimately, whatever self-confidence you build would be built on sand. It would be built on nothing because it only takes one hard fact to make your world. So, do yourself a big favor. Build your new personal narrative on sound judgments. Use facts not lies or delusions.

Chapter 12: Allow Yourself to Celebrate Daily Wins

Your judgments produce actions. I hope that much is clear. When you perceive a situation, and you fit it into your personal narrative, you come up with a judgment. The judgment is never neutral because it has an emotional component. You are triggered to respond in an emotional way, either positively or negatively. This emotional state then triggers actions. Ultimately, your judgments produce actions. Your objective observable confidence level is an action that proceeds from an internal source. Be clear about this. When you feel confident, that is an action because you allowed your emotions to have an impact on you. You either work your sense of self-acceptance, and a sense of mastery is triggered. Be aware of the fact that your feelings of self-confidence are actions in of themselves. It may not feel like you are taking action. It may seem like all of this is just taking place in your emotions, but make no mistake about it this is an action. Why?

Self-Confidence As An Action

When you feel self-confident, it is reflected in your facial expressions. It is reflected in the words you choose to express yourself. It is reflected in other signals that you send to the world. These may be non-verbal signals, but it does not matter. When you are in a certain emotional state, and it triggers a sense of confidence, you start sending out these signals you need to be mindful of this because this is you taking action on your world.

The Reality: The World is Always Judging You

Understand that when you are taking action on your world, the world is going to sit up and pay attention. As I keep repeating at the risk of sounding like a broken record, the world could not care less about your feelings. It cares about your actions. When you start taking action, you are constantly being sized up. Be mindful of your actions. Be more intentional on the signals that you send out. Choose your signals carefully. If you do, you create a positive feedback loop in terms of greater and greater self-confidence. Here is how you do it.

Confident People Act in a Way that Boosts Their Confidence Even More

When you get triggered with positive emotions, and you start acting positively; you create a feedback loop. You feel good inside. You send out good signals. The outside world acknowledges it. This can take the form of something as simple as a smile. Whatever the case may be it is some sort of outside or external validation. When you get that acknowledgment or appreciation, you then feel even better which subsequently triggers you to set even more signals out, which can then trigger another round of positive acknowledgments.

Do not let this play out randomly. Do not let this play out from time to time. It is your job to trigger this consciously, willfully and purposely. You need to build a solid feedback loop wherever you are and whatever you are doing. That is how confident people operate. That is why they are able to be confident pretty much on a 24/7 basis. They are able to do this in a conscious way that there is really not much thinking involved. They just do it like a fish takes to water.

Automatically Reading Negative Judgments Erodes Your Confidence

If you are having a tough time with self-confidence because you constantly feel that you are living in a hostile world where people are always making fun of you, degrading you, diminishing you, and otherwise discouraging you, maybe it is because you have built up a negative feedback loop.

Just as confident people have managed to build an upward spiral of increasing levels of self-confidence by working with external signals due to how they make judgments, you may be stuck in a system that works the other way. You may be choosing to pick up external signals in a way that triggers your negative personal narrative to produce negative judgments, which produce negative or stressed-out emotions. You later take action and these and just send out negative signals to the world which then bounces it back to you, and you go down another level. This keeps repeating until you go down and down and down until you feel really, really bad about yourself.

This does not have to be the case. Automatically reading negative judgments erode your confidence. Be mindful of this. This is why you need to stop yourself in your tracks. If you have a negative personal narrative, understand that you have such a narrative. Understand that you have to be more proactive in editing your personal reality.

Put simply if there are two alternative readings to a signal, pick the ones that lead to less damage. Ideally, pick the one that is either positive or, at least, is neutral. The more you succeed with this, the more and more your judgments become conscious choices. It takes getting used to. Let me tell you this is not automatic. Most people do not do things this way.

However, the more purposeful you become because you just simply opted to be more mindful of how you choose to judge signals that you see from the world, the sooner you would be able to flip the script. Instead of your interactions with the world necessarily leading to a downward spiral, you can make it go the other way around. You can make it produce an upward spiral.

Chapter 13: Practice Affirmations on Two Levels

If you are reading this book, you probably have read at least one self-help book in the past. At the very least, you most likely have become aware of a concept called affirmations; and affirmation, of course, is a statement that you say to yourself to help you mentally reprogram certain aspects of your reality. These are statements that can help you feel more effective, more successful and more confident. Mass media or Hollywood portrayals of our affirmations tend to be cheesy and cartoon-like. They often caricature people who use affirmations. Think Stuart Smalley.

Well, putting aside Hollywood's comedic or dismissive treatment of affirmations, the reason why affirmations are practiced by millions of people around the world every single day is because they work. They help you organize your reality. They help you reprogram yourself so instead of automatically assuming the worst, you consciously choose to put a positive spin on the signals you perceive from the world. Put simply, you can use these to build up your confidence.

Now here is the secret. As powerful as affirmations may be, you have to base on them on something objective. You cannot just look in the mirror and say: I am going to soar like an eagle. What does that mean? How can you do that? Do you have eagle wings? Do you have a jet pack? Do you see where I am coming from? Your affirmations have to be based on something objective in terms of your existing resources, your existing reality or your existing capabilities. In other words, you have to build them on something real.

I guess the best way to bring home the point is to compare self-affirmation with self-hypnosis. Self-affirmation basically works with what you have. For example, you like to sing, and some in the past have complemented you on your voice. Accordingly, it makes perfect sense to look in the mirror and say to yourself you are a great singer. You impact people's lives positively. You are a blessing to other people. When you say those things, you are not lying to yourself because in the past, people have complemented you on your singing skills. This comes from somewhere. It is not like you are pulling stuff out of the thin, blue air and making stuff up as you go along.

Compare this with saying to yourself you are a great singer when nobody has complimented you in the past. In fact, you yourself get annoyed at your voice because it sounds exactly like a cat being ground up in the radiator compartment of a car. In that situation, your affirmation has no objective basis.

Accordingly, you are just engaged in self-hypnosis. You are simply wishing and hoping that your waking reality would somehow be different. Now, do not get me wrong. I am not saying that self-hypnosis is a complete waste of time, and it is not worth doing. For certain people, it may work for them. For certain people, given desperate enough situations, this might be a good alternative.

However, for most people, the better approach would be self-affirmation based on reality. When you practice self-affirmation using objective evidence, you are essentially just reprogramming your mind. Your mind knows what is real and is not real. Your mind can tell between a plan and a goal, or a hope and a wish. You do not need to remind yourself. When you feed yourself affirmations that are based on reality, this increases the likelihood that your affirmations would actually build up your confidence. You would experience less resistance, and it would be easier for you to develop that upward spiral between internal confidence and external validation.

Why are Affirmations So Powerful?

Well, affirmations are so powerful because they allow you to reprogram yourself consciously. Whatever mental habits you have picked up along the way, you can deliberately rearrange them. You can intentionally "uninstall" them. You can then install new "mental software." What makes affirmation so powerful is that it is a conscious process. Compare this with how you have picked up mental habits. Chances are you have picked them up from your parents or a traumatic experience. In other words, you were not so conscious about how it happened.

However, keep in mind that it is still a choice. You still chose to hang on to that mindset; nevertheless, the whole process may have played in such a way that it was not readily apparent and clear to you. It was not clear cut. Here, everything is clear because you know what you are dealing with. You know your present reality. You know that you are not happy. You then take a different tack, and you consciously give yourself affirmations that would change your inner world. These are changes that you chose. These are changes that you have decided to implement.

Many Types of Affirmations

As I mentioned above, the Hollywood or mass media portrayal of affirmations is that it involves somebody sitting in front of a mirror and basically talking to themselves. It basically involves somebody saying you are good enough; you are good-looking; you are smart; you are intelligent; people like you. Fine, that is one way of doing affirmations. You can definitely talk to yourself in a mirror.

However, other people practice affirmations in different ways. Some use mantras. Others recite silently using mindfulness techniques. Others only simply focus on one object. For example, you are in a room at your home, and you are just staring straight ahead or you close your eyes, and you are counting your breath. Whatever the case may be there are many ways you can practice affirmation. Just because it ultimately goes down to some statement that you either speak out loud or you think about this, it does not necessarily mean that you have to sit in front of a mirror to practice affirmations.

Go Beyond Common Affirmations

There are many different ways to do affirmations and of course, the easiest is simply to come up with a list of statements that you feel would change your reality. That is a good place to start. By this point, you already have a clear idea of what your personal narrative is; you probably also would have a clear idea of certain statements that unpack or disrupt that personal narrative. When you repeat these statements, you can go a long way in changing your personal narrative and increasing your self-esteem and, by extension, your self-confidence.

However, there are many ways to skin the cat, so to speak. One way is to perceive feedback actively from the outer world, and then convert that into affirmations. For example, you are singing in a bar, and people smile at you and say you have an amazing voice. Thank you for making my night. Thank you for making me see that song in a completely different light. You cannot help but feel good. You cannot help but feel gratified by the fact that you touched somebody's life. You made a difference in somebody's life at least for that moment. You then zero in on this feedback, and you make certain judgments out of that.

You can say I am able to touch people's lives positively. I am able to make people happy. I am able to give people meaning so on and so forth. You start with a feedback, and then you convert it into an affirmation. Why is this powerful? Well, you start with the objective reality. That person actually stepped up to you and complimented you. It really happened. This is subjective reality. You can remember it. You can remember the details so you build the affirmation on top of that. These kinds of affirmations are more powerful because it is based on objective reality. It is not stuff that you think can be reasonably concluded from what you have done in the past. No, this actually happened. This is the most logical judgment of their favorable assessment of you. Do you see how this works?

That is why active perception feedback is so powerful as a form of affirmation. If you get positive feedback a lot, or if you are able to remember certain intense positive feedback, dwell on those and convert those into affirmations.

Another approach you could take is to be commentator on what is going on. Basically, you just observe the thoughts going on in your mind. You are kind of leaning back and not allow yourself to get all emotionally caught up. It is kind of like watching clouds go over head right before a storm. What you then do is you become aware that these judgments are forming, and, subsequently, you step in take control of the process. You start judging the thoughts that you begin to form in an empowering way. Instead of focusing on the negative instinctively, start looking for objectives, positive points and stick with those. Do that with one thought then another and another until it becomes a habit. This is a very powerful way of practicing affirmations because the affirmation itself does not really take the form of words; it takes the form of a mental realization.

Finally, you can position feedback you are getting from the world so that it feeds a positive feedback loop. I have already mentioned this earlier. The big difference here is that you are verbalizing the feedback loop. You are explaining to yourself in clear words what you are doing. You are saying to yourself okay that woman smiled at me. This means I am a decent-looking guy. This means I am not a threatening creep and this is a good thing. So, you kind of walk yourself in a conscious way through the process of developing a positive feedback loop.

Chapter 14: Kill the Negative Self-Talk

We all engage in self-talk. Do not fool yourself on thinking that you are completely silent inside. All of us engage in self-talk. You just have to allow yourself to catch yourself engaging in self-talk. You are always talking to yourself at some level of other. Now, this does not have to take the form of somebody who is loudly talking to themselves and having a conversation with themselves in a public area; it can be a silent thought.

You could be sitting with your friends in a bar, and somebody says something upsetting, and then you can just hear yourself inside doing an internal monologue of saying: Oh you know, what Jeff said actually refers to me. I am a bad person. Why did I do that? I could have treated that person well, but instead I chose to act like a jerk, and on and on it goes.

There is this inner monologue that is triggered by external stimuli, and you start talking yourself. Other people cannot hear, but it still takes place because you are engaged in an internal monologue. It is perfectly okay because everybody does this. In fact, according to scientific studies, people often think in a vocal way. In other words, the more they think, the further their vocal muscles get triggered. Of course, this is more acute in some people than others; however, there is a connection between our thoughts and our vocal cords. It is as if we are trying to voice out our thoughts. This happens by default.

Self-Talk is Perfectly Okay

What is important is that you become mindful of your self-talk and personal narrative. Your self-talk feeds into your self-narrative. It forms a self-reinforcing system with your personal narrative. Make sure that the personal narrative that you have consciously selected yourself, which is the personal narrative of a winner or a confident person, lines up with your self-talk. Make sure that whatever self-talk you engage in builds up your self-confidence. Make no mistake about it a lot of people engage in self-talk where they say to themselves: Oh you idiot or I screwed up; I am such a loser. You know, they often say these things to express a frustration, the event, in many cases, they express relief. Whatever the case may be; they feel like they are just letting lose.

However, let me tell you, these are not neutral words. The more you say to yourself: I have no money or I'm broke; I'm a loser; I can't do it; I'm a failure; on and on it goes; the more you re-program your personal narrative to reflect that reality. Ultimately, you reach a point where regardless of how positive the external signal may be, when you take it all in, and you fit it into your personal narrative, out comes the verdict. You are a loser. You do not have it in you. You are going to fail. Do you see how this works?

It is because you let your careless self-talk undermine your personal narrative and your self-confidence are joined at the hip. I need you to read the previous chapter regarding external signals, emotional states, judgment in actions. See how they flow into each other. Your self-talk takes place at the point of judgment and also after action. It is both a precursor and a resulting statement.

Use Negative Self-Talk Tracking to do a Mental Purge

I need you to keep a journal on your self-talk. Try to track your self-talk. In the space of a day, what are the types of statements you normally say to yourself silently? Do you say to yourself, I am a beautiful person? People like me. I am a successful person. I know how to make money. I am going places in life.

Consequently, do you say to yourself, I am a loser; I don't have any money; I'm broke. Why is life unfair, so on and so forth?

Now, I do not want you to judge your self-talk. I just need you to write it all down, track it. When you have done this for a couple of days, you should be able to see certain patterns. You should be able to see that you tend to think along definite themes. Do you look at yourself as a victim? Do you see yourself as a person that things happen to because of the past or because of people you cannot control? Or you do you see yourself as somebody who is actually an active role in making things happen.

What is important here is that you are completely honest in describing your self-talk. Do not feel that you are writing this report because you are trying to impress other people. The point is to come up with an honest assessment of how you actually think. Once you have gotten all your patterns down, and you have gotten used to writing down your self-talk, I need you to look through the record.

Be on the lookout for the following and override them consciously. I cannot emphasize this enough. Spot these issues and then the next time you engage in self-talk, be on the lookout for these and override them. The moment you spot them, override them. Disrupt them. Do whatever you need to do to prevent yourself from engaging and completing the negative self-talk process. Maybe you need to superimpose a more positive reading. Whatever the case may be, be on the lookout for negative self-talk.

Look for patterns where you feel that you deserve negative things. Look for patterns where you cast yourself in the role of victim. Look for patterns where you feel that things are merely a matter of luck, and you just happen to have a tremendous amount of bad luck. Do you see the pattern here? So, look for similar patterns and be on the lookout for them.

There is a lot at stake. When you engage in negative self-talk, and you do not check yourself, you are going to feel guilty all the time. A sense of regret will fill your thoughts or at least be a significant factor in your thoughts. You will be constantly comparing yourself to others. This is okay if you come out on the winning side, but the problem is most people who engage in negative self-talk compare themselves and set themselves up in a way that they lose the comparison.

Furthermore, when you constantly engage in negative self-talk, you fear rejection. You fear failure, and ultimately, you end up feeling that you are just flat out being judged all the time and coming up short. So, do yourself a big favor and do a mental purge of negative self-talk. I am not going to lie to you and tell you that this is going to be easy; however, it is definitely necessary. It is absolutely worth doing, and it is worth doing now.

Chapter 15: Turn Self-Confidence into a Habit

Let us be clear about one thing here. I want you to understand that "naturally" or "automatically" confident people were not born that way. While there are a small fraction that has the genetic predisposition for positivity, optimism and confidence, they are in the minority. The vast majority of people who are naturally confident learned to be that way. Understand this. It is not a foregone conclusion for you to have low self-confidence. If they can do it, you can do it, too. It may seem natural and automatic to them because they have turned confidence into a habit. You can do it as well.

How Habits Work?

So, how can you turn self-confidence into a habit? Well, first of all, you need to figure out how habits work. Habits are actually made up of three things. There is a trigger or a cue. This can be a social setting. This can be words. This can be actions taken by other people. This can actually be a lot of external signals. There are many different external signals that can work as cues.

The second part is habitual action. This does not need explaining. When you get triggered, you take this habitual action. You just feel compelled to do it. Why? Because you are looking for the third element.

The third element is when you take action, it delivers a reward. That is how you develop a habit. A lot of people smoke cigarettes right after a big meal. The trigger is the sense of fullness that they feel from their meal. This is what prompts them to whip out their pack of cigarettes and light one up. That is the habitual action. They detect the trigger, and the habitual action is they light one up. Now, what is the reward they are looking for? The reward is that the nicotine in their system constricts their blood cells so that it works with their brain chemistry to increase the sense of comfort and wellness they get from the food they just ate. That is the reward that they are looking for.

Understand that habits are always composed of these parts: cue, habitual action and reward. Confident people are able to use this system, whether consciously or unconsciously; it does not matter, to remain constantly confident.

Confident People Act Confident Out of Habit

How does this play out? Well, they detect in a certain situation that calls for confidence so, they remember to act confident. In the beginning, this takes some effort. As they get used to it, it becomes automatic, so they act confident. When they act confident, it produces a positive feedback.

For example, you go to a single's bar. There are lots of good-looking women there. You go in and you see women standing by themselves at the bar looking expectantly, and a lot of them have this neutral look on their face, and some are outright smiling at you. Out of habit, you know that this is a call for confidence. You are triggered to act more confident. You stick out your chest. You send out all sorts of positive body signals, and you step up to an attractive female giving you at least neutral signals, and you smile at her. You ask her some questions, and she responds to your questions in a positive way. She also smiles back at you. In fact, you might even see certain non-verbal signals from her indicating interest. Now, what would this make you feel? Of course, you would feel more assured. So, you feel more confident and the process starts again. You become more and more comfortable with each other. This leads to an upward spiral of greater and greater confidence and guess what, better and better performance.

This is how guys who may otherwise look very unattractive are able to hook up with good-looking women. It has nothing to do with their looks. It has nothing to do with how much money they have in the bank. It has nothing to do with any of that. Instead, it has everything to do with self-confidence. Turn this into a habit. You can turn self-confidence into a habit. It all boils down to consistent practice.

This is why it is crucial for you to always embrace and accept any opportunity to practice self-confidence. Do not run away from these opportunities. The next time you get invited to speak in front of a crowd, jump on that opportunity. Prepare for it, and then knock it out of the park. Even if you fail, that is okay. Take the next opportunity. Challenge yourself. Keep stepping up to the challenge until you achieve victory after victory. This is how you make progress.

Chapter 16: Put Together Your 30 Day Self-Confidence Building Plan

Don't get too excited. By '30 Day Self-Confidence plan', I'm not talking about you putting together some sort of 'bullet-proof' confidence building checklist that will turn you from an insecure person on Day 1 to an unstoppable highly confident person on Day 30. It's not that simple. Life is not a Hollywood movie.

Instead, I need you to take what you already know about yourself as you think about the information presented in this book. Put together a plan to start and write down realistic benchmarks you'd like to achieve on a day to day and month to month basis. Instead of expecting yourself to miraculously blossom into this amazingly confident person, take it one step at a time. Work on your self-esteem issues first. Focus on your mindsets. Layout a mindset plan for 30 days. Check your progress on Day 30.

Lay out another mindset plan for another 30 days and see if you've scaled enough to take things to a whole other level. Rinse and repeat.

By implementing your 30 Day self-confidence plans this way, you push yourself forward to greater and greater self-confidence at a realistic and sustainable pace. Don't put so much pressure on yourself that you are constantly tempted to quit. You lose when you quit. The point of these month to month 30 day programs is to focus your mind on the changes you can realistically achieve within each 30 day window.

Now, this doesn't mean you don't push yourself or challenge yourself. Quite the opposite, by laying out your timeline and proceeding to apply the points taught in this book according to the timeline, you would be able to sustainably challenge yourself to change purposefully and intentionally. You're not just chasing your tail. You're not just killing time. Instead, each day has a purpose in terms of your self-confidence goals. You then build on your progress and achievements in a sustainable and convenient way.

How many 30 day plans should you create? Answer: As many as it takes. You need to implement ALL the strategies outlined in this book. Create timelines for them keeping in mind your particular set of personal circumstances.

Conclusion

Confidence is Not Going to Appear Magically

It is a skill that you cannot learn through osmosis. You can take this book and put it right next to your head, and nothing is going to happen. Self-confidence is something that can only become a reality in your life if you seek it out and build it. In other words, you have to act on it. You cannot wait for the time to be "just right" to be confident. You cannot wait to start working on your confidence. You have to start now because tomorrow might be too late.

The good news is confidence is actually easier than you think. Why? You already have something you can be confident about. We all have passions. We all have interests. By simply choosing to nurture these passions and interests, we develop our self-esteem. The more you like yourself, the greater you find yourself worthy, the better and better your self-image becomes. You subsequently scale this up until you project it out in the form of self-confidence.

People then automatically believe that you know what you are doing. People later instantly believe that they can trust you. People subsequently believe that you are persuasive, and all of this is due to self-confidence. The good news is that you already have the raw ingredients within you to develop this kind of self-confidence. No one is such a blank slate that they have nothing to build confidence. I wish you nothing but the greatest success.

Best Regards,
Bill Andrews

FREE Mini E-Book

Thank you for reading this book. As a way of showing my appreciation, I want to give you a **FREE Mini E-Book** along with this book.

This FREE book will take you to the path of **Ultimate Life Success**. *What you'll get inside?*

3 Powerful Techniques To Power Up Your Mind In The Direction Of Wealth, Happiness & Success!!

Download URL
http://geni.us/bonusconfidence

To Read More Books By Bill Andrews, Please Visit
http://geni.us/billbooks

Printed in Great Britain
by Amazon